Uncoverings 1991

Volume 12 of the Research Papers of the American Quilt Study Group

edited by Laurel Horton

Published by the American Quilt Study Group
660 Mission Street, Suite 400
San Francisco CA 94105
Manufactured in the United States

Uncoverings is indexed by the
Clothing and Textile Arts Index and the
MLA *International Bibliography*

ISBN 1-877859-02-8
ISSN 0227-0628
Library of Congress catalog card number:
81-649486

Cover: NAMES panel made for Michael Kile
by Margaret Peters and Sally Collins, 1991.
Calligraphy by Joyce Lytle.
Fabrics courtesy of Concord and RJR.
Photograph by Sharon Reisdorf.
Cover design and production courtesy of
Kajun Graphics and The Quilt Digest Press.

Contents

Dedication: Michael Kile (1947–1991)

When I first met Michael Kile in Yellow Springs, Ohio, he had a quilt hanging on a wall of the house where he lived. His grandmother and mother had made the quilt. Quilts would hang on his walls and grace his beds for his entire life. As I got to know Michael and started buying quilts at farm auctions in Ohio, I learned that he had slept under quilts a child and even had a quilt on his bed at college. He and I took a trip to New York City in 1977 to visit a city he loved and to see quilts. We spent hours in Tom Woodard's shop looking at the most beautiful pieced Pennsylvania quilts. We couldn't believe how incredibly beautiful the 1850 to 1890 fabrics were, and we two "country boys" couldn't believe the "high" prices. We often said later we should have bought every one of them then, as prices have escalated over the years.

Returning to the Midwest, we made a concerted effort to look at quilts and learn more about them. Always the reader, and intrigued with the written word (He wrote two unpublished novels.) Michael devoured every book on quilts he could find. He took note of the fact that there were not that many from which to choose. We went to antique shops, show, and country auctions; we looked and studied and discussed what we saw. We practiced dating them; we tried to find out who had made them.

Slowly, we began to buy a few with the little money we had at the time. Not exactly knowing why, but just buying what appealed to us. Michael was very adamant about buying only those quilts which were in "mint" condition or as close to it as possible. When we eventually turned a passion into a business, his condition standards for the quilts would serve us well. We left Ohio in 1978, driving to San Francisco with a stack of quilts in the back seat of a Pontiac Tempest.

Both of us were fascinated and intrigued by the mysteries held in each quilt. We obtained as much information as we possibly could about each one. Michael wrote quilt descriptions for each quilt; the pertinent data with regard to pattern name, date, maker's name (if known), fabrics, and size. But Michael went on beyond that, sometimes two or three pages beyond that for a spectacular quilt. He always had something wonderful to write about them. I am convinced that some of our collectors bought quilts in order to get Michael's splendid quilt descriptions.

Not being satisfied to just sell quilts, Michael was always searching for other venues for creative energy. We curated exhibitions and lectured for quilt guilds where we met contemporary quiltmakers. Many of those quilt friends loved to come to our house/gallery to see the latest "finds" from a buying trip. Michael stayed current with the quilt literature and believed there was still something lacking. He felt what was missing was a quality publication which would bridge the antique and contemporary quilt worlds, a place where excellent articles by the leading people in both quilt arenas could be presented, as well as showing the finest examples of antique and contemporary quilts.

Two friends in Los Angeles had started a small publishing company with relative ease and we thought, "Why not us?" There would be many times in that first year where we would look at each other and wonder what*ever* had we gotten ourselves into! Michael's love of writing naturally had him working with the writers and content. I felt like I got the fun stuff, doing design and choosing quilts; however, Michael was doing exactly what he loved. He called in his friend Harold Nadel (who just happened to have been his college English professor) to edit that first book. The *Quilt Digest* was born.

Michael had a vision to produce the best books about quilts, be they about the history, the latest in the art quilt movement, or how to make them and choose the fabric. As the list of books published by the Quilt Digest Press attests, Michael achieved his vision.

Rod Kiracofe
1991

Preface

As this volume is edited quilts are in the national news. The Museum of American History has sold the rights to reproduce several quilts from its collection to a company which is contracting the reproductions to be made in China. This move has created a controversy on several levels. There are those who applaud the availability of affordable reproductions, others who consider the particular quilts to be national treasures and their reproduction to be a "selling out" of American values, and others who would have preferred that the quilts, if reproduced, should be the work of American craft cooperatives.

It is difficult to imagine a parallel controversy surrounding the reproduction of any other type of American expression. As Catherine Cerny states in her paper in this volume, a quilt is a "key symbol" which "represents the contribution of a group of women to the home life of a historic America, expresses the priority that women have given to family and social relatedness, and *evokes powerful emotions* from quilter and nonquilter, from women and men." This emotive power is the the issue that fuels both sides of the current controversy.

Powerful emotions also figure in Lawrence Howe's research on the NAMES Project, a movement which ironically and poignantly touches all of us in the quilt world through the death last year of Michael Kile, collector, author, publisher, and a former member of the AQSG Board of Directors. In appreciation for Michael's work, we dedicate this volume to his memory.

Two concepts related to the emotional content of quilts are *tradition* and *art*, concepts which recur in several of the papers this year. Clover Williams discovered that the quiltmakers she worked with use these terms to make distinctions within contemporary quiltmaking. William Riffe contributes to the dialogue from a very different perspective through his research on brain dominance. Most quiltmakers are familiar with the dichotomy expressed by the opposition of *tradition* and *art*, but from the discussion surrounding these papers when they were presented at the 1991 AQSG Seminar, the application or interpretation of the concepts is not a clear-cut issue.

Two new worlds of quilt research are introduced in this volume. Valerie Wilson provides us with the initial results of the Ulster quilt survey, the first opportunity most Americans have had to understand the "familiar yet different" quiltmaking traditions of the northern counties of Ireland. Closer to home, Vista Mahan presents her long-awaited study of quilts in old photographs. AQSG members over the past few years remember Vista's discovery of this overlooked subject and her requests for copies of such photographs.

Pat Nickols adds to our knowledge of important figures of quiltdom with her biographical study of Mary A. McElwain, a designer and businesswoman, whose influence forms part of the web of related quilt enterprises of the early twentieth century which we are only now beginning to explore.

Finally, AQSG is proud to include two student papers in this volume. Kyle Ciani presents an investigation into the design influences of a single significant quilt, while Caryn Kendra has researched the economic contexts influencing quiltmaking in the southern mountains. Our organization has provided opportunities for these new researchers to participate in the sharing of some of the vast informational resources represented by our membership, and to benefit from the guidance and attention pursuant to preparing their work for publication.

While previous volumes of *Uncoverings* have frequently included the works of academic scholars in a variety of fields, this year's volume may establish a new record for diversity. Scholars in American studies, home economics, organizational psychology, folklore, and history join those who are self-trained in quilt research. We join equally, because at this point the field of quilt research is so new that we are all on the cutting edge, teaching ourselves and each other things that are not yet taught through any formal instruction. We have formed a powerful and empowering network which connects us to each other, to the sources of our information, and to those who benefit from our research.

The diversity represented by our membership and by our publications reflects the many realms which are touched by quilts, quiltmakers, and textiles. Perhaps no other subject is connected to so many different fields of study. Yet, because the quilt is such a powerful "key symbol," it functions as the unifying theme to which all our work relates.

Laurel Horton
Editor

A Text of the Times: The NAMES Project

Lawrence Howe

In the category "Human Being, Anatomy and Physiology: Illness and Disease," the *Guinness Book of World Records* lists Acquired Immune Deficiency Syndrome (AIDS) with a statistical table of reported cases and numbers of deaths: the Center for Disease Control statistics are from April 1990 and report a death toll of 78,341 in the United States; by 1991 the number of U. S. AIDS deaths exceeded 120,000 and the toll is forecasted to reach 350,000 by the end of 1993. In the category of "Human achievement, Manufactured articles: Quilt," *Guinness* cites: "The world's largest quilt was made by 7,000 citizens of North Dakota for the 1989 centennial of North Dakota. It measured 85 x 134 ft."[1] In this latter citation, the *Guinness Book of World Records* is categorically mistaken; and the fact that it is wrong is all the more puzzling in light of its careful reporting of AIDS statistics. And so I begin here by correcting the *Guinness* error. The NAMES Project, the AIDS Memorial quilt, has without a doubt broken all records for the largest quilt and, sadly, continues to break its own record. This unique artifact has grown far beyond the conventional quilt as bedcover; in 1991 it was composed of over 14,000 panels, each commemorating someone who has died of AIDS, and would have filled a space equal to nine football fields. With all due respect for the collective needlework of the

---

Lawrence Howe is a Mellon Postdoctoal Instructor of American Literature at California Institute of Technology. His scholarly interests include American cultural studies, theory of the novel, African-American literature. He is currently working on a book on the relation between authority and identity in Mark Twain's novels. Division of Humanities and Social Sciences, 101–40, California Institute of Technology, Pasadena, CA 91125.

Figure 1. The NAMES Quilt displayed in Washington, D.C. © Matt Herron 1988.

citizens of North Dakota, their quilt is equivalent to about 660 panels—large, but not by AIDS Quilt standards. Re-emphasizing the sorrowful fact of what it represents, the AIDS Quilt has grown so quickly that after the display on the mall in Washington in 1989 it became logistically too difficult to exhibit in its entirety. For three years it has traveled the world in pieces. Recently, though, NAMES Project organizers and volunteers have re-evaluated both the difficulty of a full-scale exhibition and their need to make a statement in Washington about the enormity of the epidemic. In October 1992, the NAMES Project will unfold a quilt in Washington that will overshadow the 1989 exhibit, estimated to number as many as 20,000 panels and cover thirteen acres. Clearly, magnitude is a significant feature of this would-be-Guinness-World-Record Quilt with regard not only to the logistics of its display but also to its effect as an expression of grief and political outrage.

Within the quilting community, there has been debate as to whether or not the NAMES Project's artifact is a quilt at all. And the *Guinness* committee eliminated it from the quilting record because its modular assembly—consisting of eight panels stitched together into twelve foot square units to accommodate both travel and exhibition in a variety of spaces—made it in their eyes not a single object.[2] But in either case, excluding the AIDS Quilt from consideration is cause for suspicion. Despite educational campaigns, AIDS has been widely considered a disease of the gay community; in the mid 1980s one particularly uncompassionate joke that circulated through popular culture suggested that the term "gay" was an acronym for the question "Got AIDS yet?" And though there has been a shift in the demographics represented by the Quilt's panels as the epidemic's risk groups expand, the NAMES Project began in and has been largely maintained by the gay community. These challenges to the Quilt's status are not the first time that the gay community has encountered exclusion. In 1987, the U. S. Supreme Court recognized the U. S. Olympic Committee's exclusive title to the word "Olympics" and denied the right of the organizers of the "Gay Olympics" to use it for their alternative athletic competition, which as a result of the decision in that case now goes under the more ambiguous name "Gay Games." San Francisco's "Domestic partners" legislation, enacted in 1990, was challenged unsuccessfully by referendum in the November 1991 election. And historically, homosexuals have been denied access to the military because of a perceived security risk (a perception which a 1991 U. S. Army study has determined is unfounded, and in light of which Representative Garry Studds, Democrat from Massachusetts, has called for a repeal of that policy). So in a way, it is not surprising that some view the Quilt as not a quilt. However, the very issue of exclusion is a primary concern that is stitched into its composition. The AIDS Quilt is expansive not only in its physical dimensions but in the way it stretches the definition of what is a quilt. Still, if we pay too much attention to its proportions we risk overlooking the features that make this memorial a quilt—the names of the dead and the ways in which the panelmakers have sought to keep their memories alive. The Quilt is strategically exhibited to bring its viewers close to its meticulous and sometimes unorthodox handiwork: walkways lead viewers directly onto it and, if one chooses, literally in contact with the panels; and in exhibition halls where panels hang from the rafters, deck the walls, and carpet the floor, one cannot but feel that one is inside the Quilt. Both from afar and up close, we are constantly reminded that The NAMES Project is deeply rooted in the American quilting tradition.

What I intend here is to examine the Quilt both from within and from without to consider how it partakes of quilting traditions among other American traditions of representation and how it departs from those traditions, extends them, and reinterprets the ideological assumptions upon which they are stitched. I undertake this examination as neither a quilt historian nor a quilter but rather as a critic of American literature and culture. From my vantage point, the Quilt is also a text that, like all texts, reflects the emotional and ideological content of the culture in which it was produced. And the methodologies that I apply to the texts in my customary areas of study also inform the interpretations that follow here. Not unlike the Quilt itself, my observations of its textual aspects are a kind of patchwork in which I speculate on various meanings that emerge from the conception and production of The NAMES Project and the responses to it. With the seams of my observations in full view,

I hope to show how The NAMES Project is at once a quilt and a text of the times and the culture that produced it.

I begin with the question: why a quilt for this memorial? The very scope of the project would seem to make other forms of expression more likely or at least more manageable. And why a domestic craft practiced almost exclusively by women? To investigate these questions, we need to begin with another text, the story of the quilt's conceptual moment as presented in The NAMES Project's literature.

> The Quilt was first conceived in November of 1985 by Cleve Jones. A long-time gay rights activist in San Francisco, Cleve helped to organize the annual candlelight march honoring Harvey Milk and George Moscone, the San Francisco politicians assassinated in 1978. As Cleve was planning for the 1985 march, he heard that 1,000 San Franciscans had died of AIDS. To mark this terrible milestone, Cleve asked each person joining in the march to write down the names of their friends and loved ones who had died of AIDS. At the end of the march, shrouded in a sea of candlelight, Cleve and others stood on ladders taping these names to the walls of the Federal Building.
>
> In the midst of the process, Cleve stepped down from his ladder to view the growing tribute and was struck by the image of the names on the side of the building.[3]

Jones recalls, "Suddenly the names looked like a patchwork quilt, and that idea evoked such warm old memories of comfort. I had been consumed with rage and fear. Most of my old friends were dead. I felt that we lived in this little ghetto on the West Coast which would be destroyed without anyone in the rest of the world even noticing. I knew we needed a memorial."[4] One year later, Jones made the inaugural panel to commemorate his best friend Marvin Feldman.

So begins the story of the Quilt, itself a montage of thousands of other stories. The features that I would like to call attention to in this account of the quilt's inspirational moment are the mixture of emotions out of which it sprung: grief, fear, and—not least—rage; and the tangling of two different crises at its source: the first, a cataclysmic act of homophobic violence (the murders of Milk and Moscone), and the second, a growing series of quiet deaths from a neglected epidemic. In the account of Jones's inspiration, both crises are fused in a political protest that generates Jones's desire for domestic comfort, recognition, and continuity—feelings symbolized by the traditional patchwork quilt.

The emotional turmoil and the private and public utterances into which the NAMES Project channels that turmoil make quilting perhaps the most appropriate form for such a memorial. The AIDS Memorial Quilt replicates in one text the variety of motivations and expressions that mark the history of the American quilt. Gail Andrews Trechsel has written on the widespread popularity of mourning quilts in the nineteenth century either for use while observing grieving rituals or as lasting memorials of the dead.[5] And the Abolition quilts from the mid-nineteenth century, the Temperance quilts from the latter decades, the Peace Quilt project which began in 1981, and the national quilts produced for the bicentennial of the constitution were all precedents for using this domestic handicraft to make political statements. One of the aspects of the AIDS Quilt that interests me is the way that it brings different techniques together in one composite artifact and unites personal intimacy with political purpose first on a national scale and now on an international one.

This fusion of energies and intentions can be clearly seen in the panel in which Cleve Jones first materialized the inspirational concept that arose in November of 1985. Rather than a stitched artifact as the tradition leads us to expect, Jones made this panel by stenciling Marvin Feldman's name with spray paint. Thus, despite its ties to a form of Americana that has enjoyed renewed popularity in recent years, and all of the metaphors of down-home comfort that slogans like "Common Threads" and "Keep the Love Alive" consequently conjure up in the public imagination, in its genesis the NAMES Project owes at least as much to graffiti as a subversive form of political expression.

The "open panels," on which viewers of the quilt are invited to add their own messages, have made these graffiti origins part of an ongoing tradition of the Quilt's exhibition and production. Pat Ferrero and Elaine Hedges have described the importance of drawings, written sentiments, and signatures found on the friendship quilts taken on the trails of westward expansion by pioneer women, sug-

Figure 2. The open panels of the NAMES Quilt encourage visitors to add their own comments about the AIDS epidemic. © David du Busc 1991.

gesting a traditional analogue for this aspect of the AIDS Quilt.[6] In the NAMES Project, though, this technique is a way of opening up the experience of the Quilt to those who were not necessarily primary producers of panels. The "open panels" coax the audience out of passive observation into participation in the act of witnessing. When I reflect on my own experience of viewing the Quilt, it seems impossible not to be moved and not to have something to say about it and the epidemic to which it responds. The open panels not only give viewers of the Quilt an opportunity to record their responses but also draws them into the continuing creation of the project.

Some critics of the Quilt have charged that viewing it allows most Americans to dispense a little sorrow and relieve their own consciences. Michael Musto of the Village Voice has suggested that the Quilt should be tagged with a disclaimer: "Don't feel that by crying over this you've really done something about AIDS." But Jones counters that the Quilt activates people: "They come to the quilt, and they cry, and then they empty their pockets, and then they sign up and get to work. We've seen that over and over."[7] By suggesting that the audience of the Quilt is mobilized to "sign up," he verifies the success of the Quilt to achieve the goals established in 1987 and which, as the NAMES Project literature affirms, "remain the same today":

- To confront individuals and governments with the urgency and enormity of the AIDS pandemic, and underscore the need for an immediate and compassionate response, by revealing the names and lives behind the statistics.
- To build a powerful, positive, creative symbol of remembrance and hope—the NAMES Project AIDS Memorial Quilt—to link diverse people worldwide in the shared expression of our common pain, grief and rage in response to the AIDS pandemic.
- To encourage donations in every community where the Quilt is displayed, thereby raising the desperately needed funds for people living with AIDS and their caregivers.[8]

With these goals in mind, we can infer from Jones's account of this mobilization an important strategy behind the open panels. The fact that many Quilt viewers "sign up" may well be the next step after the open panels have offered them the opportunity to "sign on," demonstrating the importance of producing text to raising both consciousness and funds.

Although the Quilt expands conventional quiltmaking notions—in terms of size, concept, and technique—a large number of the panels reflect awareness for quilt traditions. The panel for Chuck Morris was made by the man it commemorates. However, having died before the Project was formed, he had no intention of contributing it to the AIDS Quilt. Rather, quilting became his own therapeutic activity for dealing with his illness. Formerly the publisher of *The Sentinel*, an activist newspaper of the San Francisco gay community, Morris withdrew from public life in 1984, two years after diagnosis. Retiring in Colorado, he learned to sew and spent two years quilting what was to become his panel. Though he died before he could complete the full-size bedcover he had planned, what he produced was precisely three feet by six feet, the size specified for panels by The NAMES Project. It was completed as a panel by Janet Lewallen, a Denver friend of Morris, who gave it a backing and decorated it with Morris's name.[9] Morris's work on the panel shows that traditional quilting patterns interested him, though the prominence of lavender and pink in the geometric design testifies as well to his willingness to improvise with symbolic colors from the gay community within the tradition he adopted.

This tendency to improvise and embellish upon quilting tradition, broadening the craft repertoire beyond convention, can be seen in a wide range of adaptations of traditional quilting technique in individual panels. With appliqué, for example, we find rather conventional uses as in the panel for Frank Feeney. Block letters spell out his name and indicate his relationship to others, his alma mater (which may have been Boston College judging from the initials and the colors), accompanied by the dates of his life, and various icons of things or ideas that the panelmaker(s) felt were important to him—knowledge, religion, music, home, and country. Or appliqué may appear in a more flamboyant style as it is in the panel for Paul Walker, in which glitter, sequins, a Mardi gras mask, and the state name "Louisiana" on a purple satin background represent the ethos of New Orleans, where Paul Walker presumably lived. Often, a photographic image is appliquéd as in the panel commemorating David

Figure 3. Patchwork by Chuck Morris which became his NAMES panel upon his death from AIDS. © Matt Herron 1988.

Lockert, who perhaps worked in broadcasting, judging from the representation of his photograph as the image on a television screen. And by interpreting the other appliquéd images we can infer that he studied or worked at Pepperdine and was fond of tennis and the telephone. Each of these panels illustrates the variety of ways in which appliqué offers suggestive clues that impel the viewer to construct interpretations of the lives commemorated.

One of the most widely used techniques in the AIDS Quilt is the textualizing of clothing. The fabrics of personal clothing of the dead were common materials of nineteenth-century mourning quilts.[10] Similarly, the double panel commemorating my brother Richard Howe and Ed Stark uses materials relevant to their lives as well as significant images. It was designed by their close friend R. Germain Fontana, an interior designer who had in recent years re-designed their house, and stitched together by a host of about twenty other friends. In designing the panel, Fontana used fabrics from draperies, upholstery, and wall coverings in their house for the background. Appliquéd to the panel is a turquoise rectangle cut from a t-shirt bearing the logo of "The Special," a Castro Street bar that Ed opened in the late sixties and which operated until July of 1991. The image of movie film and reel and the word "Hollywood" refer to Richard's interest in cinema. The brocade ribbon drawn from the reel was material used in costumes that Ed had helped make for a production of the Pacific Ballet Theatre and School for which he was a dancer and a board member. The pair of pink toe shoes in the lower left of the panel were Ed's, worn in his somewhat famous annual parodies of "Swan Lake" performed in a San Francisco, gay-community talent show that raised funds for AIDS-related charities. The pink tulle on the left and the pink satin diamond shape in the center of the panel come from the tutu that he made and wore for that role.

As in the case of the toe shoes, the AIDS Quilt quite often innovatively literalizes the materiality of appliqué in a panel's composition, flatly depicting the human forms that once inhabited a surgeon's and nurse's surgical scrubs, a police officer's uniform, a jockey's silks, a softball jersey, a postal worker's uniform, a sequined gown, a motorcycle jacket, and a favorite pair of blue jeans and a t-shirt. In this way a panel more graphically commemorates the person than by the traditional mourning-quilt technique of fashioning a geometric pattern cut from the wardrobe of the deceased. The AIDS Quilt's idiosyncratic materialized images often transcend the notion of quilting and become something more like collage, where a wide variety of personal objects are incorporated into a panel: stuffed animals, credit cards, sunglasses, feather boas, flags, phonograph records, letters, human hair, and even cremation ashes.

The point made by this collage, and the unorthodox messages that many panels bear, is that the heterogeneous materials and sometimes disarming discourse contribute to what one reviewer has sympathetically called the Quilt's "carnival of tackiness." This unconventionality, she conjectures, is "perhaps . . . the most moving and at the same time most politically suggestive thing about the quilt: the lived tackiness, the refusal of so many thousands of quilters to solemnize their losses under the aesthetics of mourning."[11] The range of expressions that the Quilt records, from passion to pathos to humor, demonstrates how quilters have unleashed their imaginations from conventions of grief and of quilting to render what Mikhail Bakhtin has called *dialogism.* This is a theory of discourse that views language as multiple, stratified, linguistic registers, based on what he calls the "heteroglossia" of language—the persistent otherness of meaning permeating language in a given context. For Bakhtin, dialogism is a literary phenomenon in which, for example, the stratified, polyvocal discourse of the novel reveals that genre to be a social text that challenges the consolidated authority of official institutions.[12] In his study of Rabelais, Bakhtin locates this subversive challenge in the festive laughter of the medieval carnival, a laughter that he describes as "gay, triumphant, and at the same time mocking, deriding. It asserts and denies, it buries and revives."[13] Obviously, the term "gay" as an adjective meaning homosexual was coined well after Bakhtin was writing, but the choice of that term derives from precisely the same impulse that Bakhtin observes in the carnival, as anyone who has witnessed Gay Pride Day festivities in recent years would attest. Moreover, the Quilt is an act of remembering buried loved ones that metaphorically revives them into memory; it functions dialogically by telling diverse stories in diverse media

Figure 4. The double panel made for Richard Howe and Ed Stark incorporates personal clothing and images from the men's lives. © Henry Faber 1991.

in order to pay respect to those who have refused to conform to the socially sanctioned model of coupling.

The use of heterogeneous materials has also long been a part of quilting. In 1829, the popular domestic theorist and abolitionist Lydia Child celebrated quilting as "The true economy of housekeeping," which she defined as "the art of gathering up all the fragments so that nothing be lost. . . . time—as well as materials."[14] The AIDS

Quilt explicitly participates in this aspect of the tradition, as well as implicitly in the liberation politics of abolitionism that Child espoused. By its inventive uses of materials, the Quilt projects an economy of excess and a celebration of disorder that runs counter to the rigid economy of conservation and order that domestic ideology prescribed for nineteenth-century quilters. But it nonetheless emphasizes a desire to gather up the fragments of lives marginalized by social disapproval of gay lifestyles in order to maintain the integrity of one of the communities hardest hit by the epidemic. Furthermore, women's quilts have themselves often projected a kind of dialogism. As many quilt researchers have noted, women stitched records of their experiences in their quilts, individually and collectively, as an alternative to officially authorized, historical discourse from which their voices were excluded. That the NAMES Project should take the form of a quilt could be seen as an appropriation of this feminine alternative discourse analogous to the way that gay men have sometimes parodied feminine behavior and adopted feminine nicknames, in the way that the Stark/Howe quilt features the nicknames "Edwina" and "Roz," as a thumbing of the nose at a society that sees them as something other than "real" men. But because of its carnivalistic gaudiness and the proportions it has assumed, the quilt demands that it be noticed in ways that nineteenth-century women's quilts rarely could. And as Marita Sturken has observed, in its openness about male love, both homoerotic and that of fathers toward their children, the quilt substitutes stereotypes of masculine stoicism with "a new kind of masculine relationship to the public display of emotion and sorrow."[15] Thus the Quilt expands not only the definition of a quilt, but also who makes quilts and what constitutes masculine attitudes and behaviors.

Some critics have seen the Quilt's implied domestic wholesomeness and the sentimentality of grief that is allied with it as a problem in the war against AIDS, and in the struggle for a national commitment to fighting that war. Observing what he sees as the Quilt's dilemma, Steve Abbott writes:

> On the one hand, the Quilt's message is positive. It personalizes the plights of PWAs [people with AIDS]; it builds support for AIDS care and fundraising; it helps break down previous stereotypes of oppressed

> communities or subculture; and it has become a bridge between communities. On the other hand, one reason the Quilt was so readily embraced by the media is because it can also be read as a memorial to a dying subculture (i.e., "We didn't like you fags and junkies when you were wild, sexy, kinky and having fun. We didn't like you when you were angry marching and demanding rights. But now that you're dying and have joined 'nicely' like 'a family in a sewing circle,' we'll accept you.").[16]

Sturken, however, refutes the idea that the "patriotism, connotation of family heritage, and sense of a larger community implied by the Quilt" has backfired, because, she contends, "the Quilt refuses to fit neatly into this narrative." Rather than "sanitizing the lives of those memorialized in the Quilt, and . . . rescripting them into a discourse of Americana in a country that has systematically rejected them as other and as people who are being punished for deviant behavior," the Quilt shows little attempt to censor quite intimate feelings about those it remembers in order to conform to some common denominator of acceptable sentiment.[17] Indeed, the Quilt's dialogical discourse, which I am arguing is a fundamental principle of its composition, represses neither grief nor anger toward governmental negligence or sluggishness in responding to the crisis. Moreover, although the Quilt originated in the gay community, many panels now commemorate women and children, and countless others were made by panelmakers who while not gay have shown their support for those affected by the epidemic.

Certainly, not everyone has come under the spell of the AIDS Quilt, as the few nameless panels attest. At least one panel admits that the name was left off by design to spare the feelings of parents who never knew or never accepted a son's gay identity, and another bears the scar of having the name effaced by family members after it was completed because they disapproved of publicizing what was apparently a stigma. But for panelmakers like Suzi and David Mandell, the AIDS quilt not only helped them overcome the loss of their hemophiliac son to AIDS but also expanded their social horizons. Suzi remembers having heard about the NAMES Project. But when invited to the Lesbian and Gay Men's Center to participate, she registered her anxiety first nonverbally by a gulp and then with the excuse that she'd have to ask her husband. With time, the Mandells' desire to do something overcame their uneasiness. Suzi recalls:

> And we had not ventured very far outside of our little middle America home into that area of the city. But we said, "Let's go." And we went down there and we found the room where they were working and met the man that I had spoke to on the phone [sic]. And I don't know, it seemed like five minutes later David was very very busy helping them out with the mailing, and I was busy stitching letters onto a person's panel. . . . Suddenly, for the first time since my son's death it was okay to laugh, really laugh.[18]

The NAMES Project is commemorative. But as Suzi Mandell's story underscores, it is also about the living, bringing disparate parts of the population together—young and old, men and women, gay and straight—making actual democratic unions out of its own analogy of stitching together motley materials. Thus as the epidemic has spread, the Quilt's diverse materials and expressions has come to signify the diverse demographics of those touched by grief as well as those who have died.

The NAMES Project also resists the implication of domestic complacency in Abbott's critical characterization of it as "a family in a sewing circle" because it refuses to lay the Quilt away in the domesticated environment of some occasionally visited museum, but rather sends it constantly traveling about the country. In essence, the Quilt is not visited by its audience but is itself a visitor, seeking out its audience by going to the communities where they live and work. The 181 displays in 1991 alone represent the kind of diverse settings in which the quilt attracts attention. To name only a few: the Apple Computer Corporate Offices in San Jose; St. Phillips Cathedral in Atlanta; the Opryland Hotel in Nashville; Ward 5B of San Francisco General Hospital; the Traverse City, Michigan, Senior High School Gym; the display window of Saks Fifth Avenue in Owings Mills, Maryland; Heritage Hall in Lexington, Kentucky; Ball State University in Muncie, Indiana; and the Convention Center-Century II in Wichita, Kansas.

As a traveling exhibition, the quilt is part of a national tradition of travel. As Barbara Brackman has observed, "Their portability and practicality made quilts and bedding among the few household items that nineteenth-century migrants were encouraged to take with them on the road west."[19] And within my concern for the Quilt as a text, it could be thought of as part of the rich tradition of American travel literature. But, for obvious reasons, in nearly all of that literature, it is not the text but the writer who does the traveling. There is a notable exception, the nineteenth-century touring panorama. The panorama, in essence, the first motion picture, was an extensive painted scene of the American landscape on a large canvas scroll that was shuttled past the audience from one reel to another. The aim was to give the effect of traveling in the same way that the 360-degree motion picture travelogue at Disneyland now takes one from coast to coast in the course of thirty minutes.[20] Except between exhibition sites and in the process of its unfolding, the Quilt does not employ literal motion. But it does figuratively call up the idea of a landscape that the audience inhabits and most importantly where those who have died of AIDS are remembered. The Quilt is a symbolic landscape that responds to the fact that those it commemorates will be missed from the actual landscape, the one in which gay men migrated from small towns to cities like San Francisco, New York, and Houston, as we can see in the panel for Keith Davis, noting his move from Oregon to New York, or in the panel for Jim Calderone, detailing his travels from Galesburgh, Illinois to college at Notre Dame, to Cincinnati, and finally to San Francisco. Their destinations were cities where neighborhoods like the Castro and Christopher Street grew, tolerance flourished, and identities were expressed without fear of oppression.

The idea of landscape has long been a part of the tradition of quilting. Thus it is not surprising to find an obvious homology between a quilt celebrating the admission of the state of Kansas to the Union and a panel in the AIDS Quilt commemorating the unnamed dead from a similar cartographic representation of counties in what appears to be Illinois.[21] As we look across the Quilt's expanse of rectangular patches, we might also think of Jefferson's plan of one-square-mile sections that became the Land Ordinance of 1785. This idealistic plan for dividing the landscape into democratic space, formed self-sufficient townships for the prosperity and self-determination of loosely joined individuals. In establishing a democratic social space that attempted to provide equality, however, Jefferson's Land Ordinance was also a legislative act of ideological will that demonstrated little sensitivity or regard for difference, human or topographical. As Philip Fisher argues, an extension of this plan is the modern American suburb so often criticized for its restraining conformity, not individuality.[22] In analyzing what they call "The Quiltmaker's Landscape," Dolores Hayden and Peter Marris note that "many American quiltmakers lived and worked in this gridded landscape. The quilt blocks they designed often were based on typical building or landscape forms defined in plan or elevation within the square grid of the quilt. The infilling of the quilt grid resembled the infilling of the survey grid."[23] They argue that a pattern like the traditional Log Cabin block quilt suggests an aerial view of such a gridded landscape no less than does Mrs. A.E. Reasoner's representation of the Delaware, Lackawanna, and Western Railroad crossing, between Hoboken, New Jersey and Richmond Springs, New York, in her 1885 crazy quilt.[24]

The AIDS Quilt appropriates this tradition and once again applies its own ideological spin. The NAMES Project's explicit rules on panel dimensions have no conscious connection to Jefferson's National Survey Legislation. In effect, the heterogeneity of the Quilt's panels show a stronger kinship to Mrs. Reasoner's violation of that gridded landscape by her use of crazy-quilt rather than symmetrical blocks to portray the landscape. Moreover, the way in which the Quilt's exhibition fills the landscape, and especially the symbolic national landscape when displayed in Washington, D.C., suggests a rejection of the urge for uniformity implicit in Jefferson's conception of the national landscape. Among its many messages, the AIDS Quilt emphatically celebrates the uniqueness of the individual and subtly suggests what more militant gay rights groups have begun to say more boldly: the epidemiology of AIDS and American demography are diverse in ways that American democracy has yet to acknowledge.

Perhaps emanating a glimmer of hope, the emphasis on social diversity in the Quilt's patchwork motif has broad congruence with emerging ideas about American culture. In 1986, American culture scholar and literary historian Sacvan Bercovitch observed a change in America's self-image. In reaction to the idea of an American literature or a national culture, he noted that many argue "that the country is sheer heterogeneity. The ruling elite has an American ideology; the people have their own patchwork-quilt (rather than melting-pot) American multifariousness."[25] Jesse Jackson, in his address to the 1988 Democratic Convention, recalled his grandmother's quilt and offered the image as a metaphor that could unite our variegated society without erasing differences. Since Bercovitch's essay, the many displays of the quilt that began in 1987, and Jackson's speech, this patchwork imagery appears to have become a prevailing paradigm: in the "Preface" to the 1991 edition of *The Heritage of American Literature*, James E. Miller, Jr. contends that instead of Crèvecoeur's "notion of the new country as a 'melting pot,' the contemporary imagination is more likely to compare America to a varicolored patchwork quilt."[26] Certainly, the AIDS Quilt is influenced by and in turn influences that contemporary imagination and thus is, as I have called it, a text of the times.

Yet, to give that phrase a slip of the tongue, it is also a test of the times, a very serious and urgent test for people who don't have much time left. The debate over multiculturalism in which Bercovitch, Jackson, and Miller participate will no doubt have real political, educational, and social consequences in the future, but the war on AIDS and on discrimination against people with AIDS that the Quilt seeks to publicize is a battle for the future that some will not live long enough to see. And this is where the Quilt's terrible, growing expansiveness is most significant. In the Quilt film *Common Threads*, Vito Russo, one of the featured storytellers, forecasts

> an end, a day when we can stop adding panels to this quilt and put it away, as a symbol of a terrible thing that happened that's now over. You know we forget that someday this is going to be over. Someday there's going to be no such thing as AIDS. And people will just look back and remember that there was a terrible tragedy that we survived.27

Earlier in the film, Russo addresses a crowd of demonstrators at an AIDS rally in New York and explains that he is there because he doesn't want to end up as a name "on a Quilt in front of the White House." If only his hopeful and courageous eloquence were enough—the Quilt has not been put away, and in 1991 a panel for Vito Russo helped the Quilt extend its unacknowledged record. In the case of the NAMES Project, America's penchant for doing things big, for outdoing itself, indeed for even keeping track of things like largest quilts, has, to say the least, stretched more than one tradition.

Acknowledgments

For their ideas, images, and support, I would like to thank Michelle Cinqmars and Scott Osten at the NAMES Project, David du Busc, Henry Faber, Randy Fontana, Judy Frei, Matt Herron, Marita Sturken, Cindy Weinstein, and the Graphic Arts Department at Caltech. All images used by permission of the photographers and the Names Project Foundation.

This essay is dedicated to the memory of Richard Howe and Ed Stark.

The American Quilt Study Group wishes to thank the Northern California Quilt Council for their generous donation toward the publication of Lawrence Howe's paper.

Notes and References

1. McFarlan Donald, ed. *Guinness Book of World Records* (New York: Bantam, 1991), 35–36, 489.
2. Confirmed in a telephone conversation (January 1992) with Maria Morgan, Deputy Editor of the *Guinness Book of World Records.*
3. "Background: The NAMES Project AIDS Memorial Quilt," (The NAMES Project AIDS Memorial Quilt, San Francisco, February 1991), 1–2.
4. Quoted in Dan Bellm, "Cleve Jones: And sew it goes," *Mother Jones* 14 (January 1989): 35.
5. "Mourning Quilts in America," in *Uncoverings 1989*, ed. Laurel Horton (San Francisco: American Quilt Study Group, 1990), 139–58.
6. *Hearts and Hands: The Influence of Women and Quilts in American Society* (San Francisco: Quilt Digest Press, 1987), 33.
7. Bellm, 35.
8. "Background," 2.
9. Cindy Ruskin, *The Quilt: Stories From The NAMES Project* (Pocket Books: New York, 1988), 27.
10. Trechsel, 144.
11. Elinor Fuchs, "The AIDS Quilt," *The Nation* 247 (October 31, 1988): 408–9.

12. M. M. Bakhtin, "The Discourse of the Novel," in *The Dialogic Imagination*, ed. Michael Holquist, trans. Caryl Emerson and Michael Holquist (Austin: University of Texas Press, 1981), 259–422.
13. *Rabelais and His World*, trans. Helene Iswolsky (Cambridge: MIT Press, 1968), 11–12.
14. Quoted in Ferrero and Hedges, 26.
15. "The AIDS Quilt: A Memorial as Testimony," paper presented at the California American Studies Association Conference (April 1991), 10.
16. "Meaning Adrift: The NAMES Project Quilt Suggests a Patchwork of Problems and Possibilities," *San Francisco Sentinel* 16.2 (October 14, 1988): 24.
17. Sturken, 12. I have Marita Sturken to thank for much of what I know about the controversies that have sprung up around the strategies of The NAMES Project: either for politicizing the Quilt, thus violating the intentions of the panel makers and disrespecting their expressions of grief, or for not being political enough and accommodating "middle America" and helping assuage the guilt of their neglect.
18. *Common Threads*, dir. Robert Epstein and Jeffrey Friedman, Telling Pictures and The NAMES Project Foundation, 1989. Motion picture.
19. "Signature Quilts: Nineteenth-Century Trends" in *Uncoverings 1989*, ed. Laurel Horton, (San Francisco: American Quilt Study Group, 1990), 26.
20. See Barbara Novak, *Nature and Culture: American Landscape and Painting, 1825–75* (New York: Oxford University Press, 1980), 23–28.
21. Ferrero and Hedges, 54; Ruskin, 80.
22. See Philip Fisher, "Democratic Social Space: Whitman, Melville, and the Promise of American Transparency," *Representations* 24 (Fall 1988): 60–101.
23. "The Quiltmaker's Landscape," *Landscape* 25 (1981): 45.
24. "The Quiltmaker's Landscape", 42.
25. "Afterword" in *Ideology and Classic American Literature*, ed. Sacvan Bercovitch and Myra Jehlen, (Cambridge: Cambridge University Press, 1986), 436–37.
26. "Preface," *The Heritage of American Literature*, 2 vols, ed. James E. Miller, Jr. (New York: Harcourt Brace Jovanovich, 1991), I: v.
27. *Common Threads*.

A Quilt Guild: Its Role in the Elaboration of Female Identity

Catherine A. Cerny

The paper addresses the symbolic dimensions of the modern quilt world by analyzing how the activities of a quilt guild structure women's understanding of quilt tradition and consequentially shape their expressions of self, life experiences, and social relationships through quiltmaking. Such an interpretive orientation requires both documentation of guild activities and analysis of what participants gain from their involvement. To meet this purpose, I conducted fieldwork with Minnesota Quilters Inc., located in the metropolitan areas of St. Paul and Minneapolis where most of the 850 members resided and most of the activities occurred.[1] Observations were made over a twelve month period, between September 1984 and September 1985. At the time of this study, membership was predominantly female; the few male members occasionally attended lectures but did not participate actively in guild leadership or events.

One way of understanding the symbolic dimensions of community is through ethnographic analysis of the social setting. Shared values and attitudes become apparent as they affect the interactions and discourse of public activities. The purpose of ethnography is to describe a culture from the perspective of the people who comprise the community. This ethnographic study is premised by the view that how a community defines this culture is crucial to any explana-

---

Catherine A. Cerny is an assistant professor at the University of Rhode Island and teaches undergraduate and graduate courses in the social psychology of dress. Her research interests include the social history of quiltmaking in Rhode Island and the cultural significance of wedding dress. Department of Textiles, Fashion Merchandising and Design, University of Rhode Island, Kingston, RI 02881.

tions of behavior. Careful observation of a community, with attention to group activities and interactions, is necessary to reveal the meanings that shape individual perceptions and behaviors. Fieldwork positions the ethnographer within a community and provides the tools to observe, record, and draw inferences from the more concrete manifestations of the culture (including social events, conversations, publications, and material goods). The ethnographer reasons from the evidence and tests these inferences throughout the fieldwork experience until certain that hypotheses represent accurate and logical explanations about the phenomena. This orientation allows the ethnographer to enter the fieldwork situation with minimal preconceptions about a culture, to observe the daily activities of the community and attend to the perspectives of participants, and, finally, to generalize about the relevance of the phenomenon to community life.

In the following discussion about quilt culture, I speak about the success of the guild in providing a women's support group that addresses and partly resolves the ambiguities of contemporary female social life by elaborating a traditional female identity. I develop the analysis first by characterizing the modern quilt guild as an example of "feminine culture," second by defining the mechanisms inherent in guild activities that communicate meaning to the guild member, and finally by documenting the quilters' appropriation of these meanings through their quiltmaking.

Feminine Culture: The Example of Minnesota Quilters

The quilt guild reconstructs traditional values of female life in late-twentieth-century society. The modern guild can be qualified as an extension of the nineteenth-century quilting bee experience. Quiltmaking was and continues to be an opportunity for women to socialize within a setting in which a "feminine culture" dominates. Similarly, the modern quilt guild has a culture that can be distinguished as a community of women. Yet the guild is also a community that defines its identity by juxtaposing sentiments toward a past with realities of the present, and a community, though bound by common interests, that provides options for individual expression.

In the book *The Feminization of America*, Lenz and Myerhoff characterize a traditional "feminine culture" that is fundamentally transient; although centered on the family, the culture is shared through the common experience of being a woman. Women assume "responsibility for matters dealing with the quality of life, with relationships and relatedness; with emotions and diffuse, universal concerns—the whole human being."[2] Their energies are devoted to the process of daily living: "the producing of children; the care for the sick and dying; the nurturance of the elderly; the gathering, cleaning, and preparation, and serving of food; the tending of hearth and home; the sweeping, sponging, chopping, mending, wiping that is ceaseless and evanescent."[3] These priorities shape a feminine identity characterized by "a strong nurturing impulse that extends to all living things; . . . a tendency to integrate rather than separate; an ability to empathize;. . . . an attachment to the day-to-day process of sustaining life; . . . a scale of values that places individual growth and fulfillment above abstraction."[4] Under these circumstances, women developed a "distinctive sensibility, a style of life, set of values, as well as activities, relationships, and cognitive and emotional predilections," which become apparent in their interactions with other women.[5] Lenz and Myerhoff suggest furthermore that such female experiences have contributed to an interpersonal style of "cooperative individualism," in which self-interests merge with that of the group. Through the mutual cooperation and support provided by women's friendships, the individual is empowered to meet the circumstances of her life.

The example of Minnesota Quilters Inc. demonstrates an elaboration of this notion of a community of women, one which partly appropriates the tactics of a business world to optimize opportunities for its members' experience of quilt tradition. The guild was founded in 1977 and incorporated in 1978. A board of fourteen elected members, assisted by appointed committees, oversees the annual schedule of events. These events include monthly membership meetings (day and evening), biennial lecture-workshop series by nationally known quilters, a fall weekend retreat, and a spring quilt show and symposium. In addition, the guild publishes a monthly newsletter and manages a circulating library.

One of the larger quilt guilds in the United States, Minnesota Quilters can be seen as an umbrella organization that has drawn together individual quilters and independent community-based guilds and circles from throughout the state and made them part of a regional network. Minnesota Quilters has expanded opportunities for these women by utilizing the knowledge and skills of its diverse membership, while supporting the smaller circles where the intimacy of the "quilting bee" is sustained. By establishing a network that connects the local quilter with national and international happenings (i.e., workshops and lectures by nationally recognized instructors, newsletter announcements of symposiums, and lectures about quilters/needleworkers of other cultures), the guild has further consolidated the community and lent increased validity to individual members' involvement in quiltmaking. Thus in this context, women's achievement is defined and validated from a female perspective.

For some, quilts may evoke images of female dependency in a male-dominated society. Yet, by viewing the quiltmaking revival of the 1970s in relation to a concurrent revival in feminism, this stereotype can be challenged. The women's movement of the 1960s and 1970s promoted the idea of networking to afford women the same mentoring advantages of an "old boy" network and thus to empower women within male-dominated business circles. Lenz and Myerhoff note, however, that these women's networks, by being based in a tradition of female friendships, were unlike male networks.[6] Women's groups provide mutual support within a context of "warmth and emotional openness." The example of modern quiltmaking is particularly interesting for its inclusion of imagery from an almost mythic past. For example, quilt tradition can evoke the circumstance of "pioneer women" who, despite the remoteness of rural America and their daily struggle for survival, established support groups that not only helped them cope with their harsh existence, but through their quiltmaking brought beauty to the foreign environment. Today, the contemporary quilt guild draws upon this collective mythology, as women nurture each other with the self-confidence necessary to face the realities of post-industrial society.

Minnesota Quilters exemplifies a "feminine culture" by offering its members a supportive setting structured in large part by values consistent with traditional priorities of home and family. The extent and nature of participation in MQ events varies with the individual member, the circumstances of her life, and her orientation to quiltmaking. The nature of the organization and scheduling of activities has allowed the guild member many options: The more active member might serve on the board of directors or volunteer for a committee, teach a workshop, take classes, and display a quilt at the annual quilt symposium. The less active member might attend one or two monthly meetings, share a finished quilt during show-and-tell, and take a workshop during a special event.

I developed a three-page questionnaire to address questions about demographic background of members, their involvement in quiltmaking, participation in Minnesota Quilters, and interests in quilted patchwork apparel, based on initial observations of the guild and in-depth interviews with nineteen members (including founders of the guild, current board members, teachers, and others).[7] This questionnaire was distributed during the four days of the 1985 symposium. One hundred seventy questionnaires, representing twenty percent of the membership, were returned. While this method of distribution might have biased the results in favor of the more active participants, actual results indicated that the sample included members with varied rates of attendance at meetings and involvement in guild educational and volunteer activities.

Evidence drawn from the questionnaire supports the view of quilters as women whose personal experiences are rooted in family life. Members ranged in age from the late twenties to over seventy. Eighty-six percent were married; four percent, widows; three percent, separated or divorced; and only six percent were single. Eighty-five percent had children; thirty-five percent had grandchildren. Eighty percent considered themselves homemakers; however, at the same time, seventy-four percent indicated they were employed part time or full time.

A similar orientation toward quiltmaking was suggested by the respondents. Although they acknowledged interest in both traditional and contemporary quilting styles, they preferred the traditional format. Three percent expressed an preference only for traditional quilts; forty-eight percent preferred traditional quilts; thirty-nine percent liked traditional and contemporary quilts equally; five percent preferred contemporary quilts; and no respondent liked only contemporary quilts. Likewise among the respondents, sixty-six percent preferred hand applique; fifty-eight percent, hand piecing; eighty-eight percent, hand quilting; and nine percent preferred machine applique; fifty-four percent, machine piecing; and eight percent, machine quilting.

In the same survey, members responded to what was special about being a Minnesota quilter.[8] In diverse ways, members contextualized their identities as a "Minnesota quilters" in terms of the broader "feminine culture," described by Lenz and Myerhoff. One of these quilters characterized this linkage as "the fellowship with women of all ages from which inspiration flows." In addition, members understood inherently that a cooperative interpersonal style was the basis of the individual's creativity and that with nurturing, the individual was empowered. This awareness was revealed through the priority given to "inspiration" and "stimulation to try new things" in their identification as Minnesota quilters. Furthermore, although unrelated by family ties and often dissimilar in social background, Minnesota Quilters, nevertheless, has attracted women to a community, which like any culture, has a common language. We see this recognition by the membership: women noted the camaraderie of women who "speak the same language." Quiltmaking is a cultural setting which has accommodated the needs of women who may see themselves as uncomfortable with the ambiguities otherwise present in post-industrial society. One quilter noted that Minnesota Quilters was the "only place I am understood!" Another clarified the benefits of being part of this community:

> It is a group of people who can appreciate your interest and have understanding for the sorts of problems you may encounter. (Like a mother with small children feels better knowing that other kids do what hers just did even though the problem was not resolved.) There is comfort in knowing you are not alone and the support and encouragement of

> those with similar interests is more meaningful than groundless praise of those who have never had the experience.

The understanding that comes from shared experiences, whether it reflects what women share in managing the family or what they share in tackling the challenge of quiltmaking, contributes to a woman's sense of satisfaction with self and accomplishment in her endeavors. Mutual support gained from membership helps not simply with quiltmaking, but with struggles in coping with life.

At a time when economic pressures are fragmenting domestic life, the distinctive culture of quiltmaking has established a community in which more traditional female values can be represented and affirmed. However one also must recognize that this femininity is not a fixed image within the modern guild. There is a persistent, albeit subtle, tension between the more traditional and more contemporary definitions of the female identity. The negotiations that occur in the day-to-day activities of the guild reflect the overriding ambiguity of women's roles in late twentieth-century American society as women seek to "have it all," to fulfill obligations of family life, and to gain recognition for individual achievements. Similarly, one must acknowledge as well that this tension has long been part of women's needlework. Scholars, such as Macdonald and Parker, have argued that women's domestic textiles have provided the means to negotiate femininity in a society governed by a patriarchal ideology.[9] Langellier finds that, for contemporary quilters in Maine, quiltmaking empowers the women by re-fashioning femininity around modern circumstances of family, work, and leisure.[10] Similarly in Minnesota, the quilt guild provides the social context within which members can draw upon the values of a women's tradition to elaborate feminine dimensions of self.

Guild Activities: The Nurturing of Women within a Context of Tradition

All guild activities can be equated as rituals through which the meanings embodied by the quilt are elaborated for the benefit of the quilter. By grounding the quilter in a women's history, the guild characterizes the values and attitudes that lead to a more traditional female identity. The display of antique quilts and the stories of nineteenth-century quilters celebrate the virtues and achievements of "pioneer women," at once independent and bound to family, and promise this integrity of self to the modern quilter. Correspondingly, by elaborating contemporary options through lectures and workshops, the guild promotes the shaping of an identity that is both consistent with the ideology and authentic to personal goals.

Lectures (the focus of monthly meetings and featured during the annual symposium) reconstruct the historical, cross-cultural, and modern dimensions of quilt and parallel textile traditions. Through descriptions of the social experiences and accomplishments of female quilters, the speakers delineate core values of "feminine culture." The display of the quilt, whether as slide or actual object, adds emphasis to the discourse. Many of these presentations focus on local and nationally recognized quiltmakers. In self-portraits, the women suggest how they have been able to balance family and professional life. The speaker's quilts are juxtaposed to significant events or accomplishments in her life. References to specific technical and artistic features suggest corresponding qualities of femininity, with which the audience can identify. As suggested by Lenz and Myerhoff, these qualities center on nurturing the individual through social integration. Programs, held as an alternative to more instructional demonstrations, point out, albeit subtly, the symbolic potential of a quilt expressing individual feelings, relationships, and experiences. The woman gains an understanding of how she can similarly individualize her quiltmaking, create a quilt that has significance, and achieve satisfaction from the experience. At the same time, she gains perspective on who she is as quilter, and consequently as woman.

Workshops (featured four times during the year during workshop/lecture series, fall retreat, and spring symposium) and instructional lectures place the woman as part of quilt tradition. They detail the processes by which feelings, relationships, and experiences become expressions. Workshops provide hands-on instruction and focus on the student's mastering specific quiltmaking techniques and/or design strategies. Classes address practical procedures in pattern drafting, piecing, quilting, and basic design principles necessary in rendering or adapting historic quilt patterns. Instructors focus on specific technical and design topics: short-cut methods for piecing and quilting, innovative strategies for interpreting traditional patterns, nonwestern and other artistic techniques adapted to the quiltmaking process, or aesthetic considerations in modifying a block pattern for alternative quilted items. Much of the instruction is presented in a manner meant to develop the student's creative skills. Instructors demonstrate a range of options through slide shows or samples and then work closely with students as they select fabrics, modify patterns, or develop original designs to fit their specific purposes.

Whether through lectures or workshops, the instructors establish quiltmaking as a creative process in which the opportunity for personal expression lies within the domain of a quilt aesthetic system. They illustrate how the quilter can work within quilt tradition, not simply to duplicate a pattern or to reinterpret a traditional pattern, but to utilize this knowledge to express personal tastes and experiences. This potential can be readily seen with the example of the Log Cabin quilt and in the teaching strategy of the instructor. Through slides of historic and contemporary quilts, Joanne Holzkecht described the potential variants of the Log Cabin pattern during an evening program on September, 1985. Within this range, no single Log Cabin quilt is like another. The quilter's choices with respect to fabric and color use within each block and to the block arrangement on the surface yield the unique design. Furthermore, alternatives to the traditional format showed contemporary quilters how they can break from traditional formats to create pictorial images. In the subsequent newsletter report on the program, the reporter noted, "It is such great fun to see what fresh things can be done with such a traditional pattern when clever quiltmakers use their rich imaginations."[11]

Whereas lectures expose guild members to the range of quiltmaking techniques and designs and allow them to recognize stylistic preferences, workshops provide the guidance required to refine a personal style of expression, which is indicative of a more global self. Knowledge of quilt tradition is central to this process as the woman sorts out the meanings to differentiate relative qualities of femininity (especially in terms of family relatedness and individual integrity). Being traditional or contemporary can be equated as an attitude suggested by the quilter's choices. Traditional style is that which is learned and adopted through observation of historic quilts. Traditional designs have meaning due to the names attributed to patterns at some point in the historic past, although the interpretations of these meanings are mediated by modern circumstances. Quiltmakers' handstitching techniques in piecing or appliquing the pattern and quilting the design similarly qualify meaning.

Contemporary styles are derived from the traditional patterns, techniques, and uses. However innovative, the quilter refers to the aesthetic principles established by her predecessors. Indeed, such innovation is part of the tradition. Since the nineteenth century, contemporary quilters have instilled personal experience in the characterization of traditional design by selectively transposing and/or modifying established patterns and techniques and by renaming the design. With an understanding of the nineteenth-century tradition of quiltmaking, today's contemporary quilter has more options, whether in the end use of the item or in the innovations of technique and design. Some may even expand the boundaries of the quiltmaking aesthetic as they explore broader artistic issues.

A more traditional orientation to quiltmaking implies a preference for a more historic expression of femininity in which women's achievement is defined largely through familial relationships within a domestic setting. A more contemporary orientation implies a desire to break free from this ideology and to define a self more in tune with the changing times. However, these are simple generalizations. The reality of postmodern times does not allow for easy, unambiguous answers.

The Displayed Quilt: An Expression of Female Identity

The meanings inscribed through quiltmaking are revealed as the Minnesota Quilter speaks about her quilts. Opportunities to "show-and-tell" a quilt occur throughout all the events of the guild: on a conversational level as women get together during the fall retreat, in workshops as students share their works-in-progress, and as a regular feature of the monthly meetings. On a more formal scale, show-and-tell has its equivalent in the modeling of apparel during a fashion show or in the exhibit of quilts during the annual symposium. In the latter case, members can refer to a catalog that contains descriptions written by the quilter or owner. The telling about the quilt, its design, making, and/or use are especially revealing as the woman documents her achievements, from concurrent perspectives of quilter and woman.[12] Statements from the "Scrap Quilt Magic" exhibit catalog illustrate how the quilter draws upon traditional patterns, such as the Log Cabin block, and reinterprets the designs to elaborate on personal experiences.[13]

First of all, through her comments about the quilt, the woman positions an identity as quilter with references to a quiltmaking lifestyle, aesthetic traditions, and social relations established within the quilt community. Maintaining a quiltmaking lifestyle necessitates balancing quiltmaking interests with other social responsibilities. Public reflections on personal experiences point out common difficulties and suggest ways of overcoming everyday obstacles to quiltmaking.

> This was my first pieced quilt—started as a pillow out of the scraps from my maternity clothes. The pattern came from Ickis and I quilted it using the "quilt-as-you-go" method.[14]

The quilter, by revealing moments from her personal life, suggests that like quiltmakers from both past and present, she is making judicious use of fabric through recycling of scraps from her maternity clothes. Secondly, not only does she note that this is her first quilt and that it was made in a particular manner, but she implies a growing confidence in her skills as the pillow is transformed into a bedcover.

Many comments highlight the women's ingenuity in solving construction or design problems and in personalizing the quilt design. A woman's knowledge of quilt tradition encompasses a range of technical, design, subject matter, and use possibilities. Working within this framework, the quilter defines significance in terms of her aesthetic choices: "Red center for warmth in the home. Twenty-three different fabrics used, some old and some new."[15] Although brief, the statement reveals a understanding of the symbolic potential of quilts. First, the quilter demonstrates her understanding of the concepts of the scrap quilt; she indicates the number of different fabrics used and that they included both old or new. Second, she evidences her knowledge of a quilt rhetoric based in the home and family; the use of red color, its placement at the center of each block, and its use with the Log Cabin pattern enhance the emotive power of the quilt.

The guild member's socialization as a quilter is marked by a commitment to quiltmaking and an affiliation with other quilters. The displayed quilt represents the woman's desire and efforts to be recognized within the quilt community:

> I purchased the fabric five years ago, and planned to learn to quilt when I had lots of time in my old age. I decided I couldn't wait that long, not to mention the probable need for tri-focals by then to see the stitches. So I took a class from the "Quilt Block" [quilt shop]. Two and a half years later, it has traveled through 13 states and infected 12 other women with the "disease of the needle."[16]

In this case, the Log Cabin block is one of many blocks in this Sampler Quilt. The quilter attributes the significance of this quilt to her beginnings as a quilter and growing connectedness with quilters; the quilt provides the opportunity to share with others the pleasures, if not the frustrations of quiltmaking.

What we see implied in the above statements is the extent to which the tradition of quiltmaking can potentially interplay with a woman's day-to-day activities. Whereas the quilt guild represents the values from a vague past and demonstrates their relevance to the present, the quilter integrates them as part of her experience through the course of designing and making a quilt. The implications and consequences of this activity are revealed as the quilts become an opportunity to speak about a life beyond the quilt guild.

The guild members' comments simultaneously elaborate on their roles as women in American society. Quiltmaking, as an expressive activity, does more than situate each member within the quilt subculture: It defines her position with respect to the larger social environment, that of family and women, over time and in the present. The women's statements suggest that these relationships are defined both in the process of quiltmaking (i.e., source or inspiration of the design, assistance in its making), and through the use of the quilt as gift (i.e., mark special event in the recipient's life).

The women elaborate on family relationships by describing the circumstances of a quilt's design, construction, and/or use. On the one hand, family members (including husband, sister/brother, daughter/son, grandchild, cousin, or parent) assist with selecting the fabrics and patterns and help with piecing or quilting. On the other hand, the quilter selects the design that relates to the interests of a recipient. In either case, the quilt acquires significance through the other's actual or imagined involvement in the making. For example, the mother-daughter bond is perpetuated even after the daughter reaches adulthood:

> My daughter picked out the fabric; I cut out the quilt and sent the pieces to her to sew. She ended up sending them back to me and I ended up making the quilt. It is made of burgundy and greys with [T]hinsulate batting and is machinequilted.[17]

Although now living apart from the daughter, the mother was able to establish a relatedness through the daughter's selection of fabric for the quilt and, to some extent, continue a dialogue as the quilt is sent back and forth through the mail.

In a similar manner, the quilt elaborates on the community in which relationships with men or other women extend beyond the family domain. The modern quilter maintains the tradition of the friendship quilt which acknowledges mutual interests and the quilt made for charity which acknowledges a responsibility to community welfare. The example of a friendship quilt is reflected in the following case:

> This was machinepieced and machinequilted and made using a variation of "quilt as you go"—the front is machine stitched while the back is hand whipstitched. I made this Log Cabin quilt originally for myself but when my friend Ken saw it he fell in love with it. I am surprising him with this quilt when the show is over. It has taken me three years to finish this quilt; the body was finished fairly quickly but I couldn't decide on the border. After two years of thinking about it (and with the help of my friends Ken and P.J.) I decided on the borders.[18]

The example of a quilt made for charity is reflected in the following case:

> This quilt is a study in traditional quilt blocks, made from blue and muslin all-cotton fabrics. Each quilt guild member made a block of her choice and then contributed time for the quilting. The quilt top was assembled by guild member Colleen Nelson. The quilt was made to give members a common experience in quiltmaking. It will be donated to Winona Community Memorial Hospital to serve as a wallhanging in the Family Room of the obstetrical department.[19]

Underlying the significance of each quilt is an understanding of the quilt as metaphor of solidarity, as fragments of fabric are pieced together so are the relationships that the quilter has within society. In the case of the former statement, the finished quilt manifests the bond of friendship between the quilter and Ken. In the case of the latter statement, the quilt has drawn together women who share an interest in quiltmaking but demonstrated their sense of responsibility to the community.

The meaning of quilted objects derives initially from their identity as bedcoverings. Traditionally, the bedquilt has been associated with home and family and with the role of the woman in maintaining the domestic unit. The quilt's use within the household or as gift to a relative strengthens family bonds. This theme has carried over to contemporary derivation of the bedquilt and qualifies significance in modern terms. As the social network of modern women expands and becomes more complex, so too does the signifying function of quilts become more circumstantial. As demonstrated in the above examples, women can use the quilt to mark social affiliations in very specific ways. At the same time, quilters can make quilts that are used beyond familial, friendship, and charitable domains, for financial gain and artistic recognition. The quilter's descriptions of aesthetic choices and attributions of meaning demonstrates the importance in highlighting individual creativity and resourcefulness.

The Quilt as Symbol: Implications in the Elaboration of Identity

Interpreting the meaning of quiltmaking within the context of the guild necessitates recognition of the centrality of the quilt in the community of quiltmakers. Most of us would acknowledge that the quilt is a symbol. A symbol is generally understood as "something chosen to represent something else; especially, an object used to typify a quality, abstract idea, etc."[20] However, this definition does not do justice to the powerful emotions the quilt generates within American society. The meanings associated with the quilt are complex; significance extends beyond simple representation of idea—a warm bedcover made principally by women for use by family members.

The quilt is the key symbol of the quilt subculture.[21] It "summarizes" quilt tradition by synthesizing the life experiences of nineteenth-century women and relating these as values to modern society. By virtue of its form, the quilt represents the contributions of a group of women to the home life of a historic America, expresses the priority that women have given to family and social relatedness, and evokes powerful emotions from quilter and nonquilter, from women and men. As a totality, quilts constitute a visual record of female social life and occupation, parallel to the written history of male-dominated society, and define an otherwise diverse, dispersed community of women. At the same time, the quilt potentially "elaborates" on the quilter's experience as a woman; the quilt and quiltmaking serve as means for "sorting out complex and undifferentiated feelings and ideas, making them comprehensible to oneself, communicable to others, and translatable into orderly action."[22] The quilt embodies a belief structure around which the subculture of quilters is defined. The values and modes of behavior, associated with the traditions and myths of quiltmaking, are activated and provide models of a feminine lifestyle. In these terms, quiltmaking "participates in a re-fashioning of femininity that is personally and socially empowering."[23]

Today we can understand the quilt as both summarizing and elaborating upon a tradition of quiltmaking. However, the dominance of one meaning over the other in structuring perceptions varies with individuals and their respective circumstances. For most Americans, seeing the quilt in the bedroom of a home recalls the warmth one feels within close-knit family. The intensity of emotion felt upon recognition of the quilt is a consequence of its association with an image of some idealized past. This meaning comes out of our appreciation of the quilt and stories about the quiltmaker. However in some cases, the quilt plays a more intimate role within a person's life. By summarizing tradition, the quilt is essential to understanding the dynamic by which quilters, especially women quilters, elaborate a female identity. In this case, their involvement in quiltmaking becomes the opportunity to express feelings and attitudes about one's self, life experiences, and relationships to others. It is this latter perspective on the symbolic nature of the quilt that I addressed through my observation of a quilt guild. Today the quilt guild is but one facet of quilt culture (others include quilt periodicals, instructional manuals, exhibition catalogs, international conferences, and quilt-related businesses) that enhances this transposition of meaning from an abstract value to concrete experience.

As a manifestation of "feminine culture," Minnesota Quilters provides the sociocultural context within which members can identify with and integrate quiltmaking as part of their social life. Through identification as quilter, a woman can re-affirm traditional values as well as delineate individuality as a female. As the woman becomes knowledgeable about quilt culture and is socialized as a quilter she can enact a lifestyle that balances traditional definitions of being female with modern circumstances. Knowledge of quilt culture enables the woman to implement the identity of a quilter and to achieve expression that elaborates on roles as wife, mother, grandmother, daughter; as friend and colleague; and potentially as artist, entrepreneur. In turn, the understanding and support that a woman receives with the display of the quilt can reinforce self-concept and enhance self-esteem.

Acknowledgments

The American Quilt Study Group wishes to thank the New England Quilters Guild for their generous contribution toward the publication of Catherine Cerny's paper.

Notes and References

1. Since 1985 the guild has continued to grow; by the end of 1990, membership numbered 1,100. Carol Wagner, letter to author, December, 1990.
2. Elinor Lenz and Barbara Myerhoff, *The Feminization of America: How Women's Values are Changing our Public and Private Lives* (Los Angeles: Jeremony P. Tarcher, 1985), 7.
3. Ibid., 6.
4. Ibid., 4.
5. Ibid.
6. Ibid., 57–74. Lenz and Myerhoff discuss the origins of networking among women and trace this to contemporary strategies that enhance women's power in public affairs.
7. Catherine A. Cerny, "Quilted Apparel: A Case Study of a Cultural Vehicle" (Ph.D. thesis, University of Minnesota, St. Paul, 1987), 74–105.
8. The quoted statements in this paragraph are drawn from anonymous responses to the open-ended question on the questionnaire, "What is special about being a Minnesota Quilter?" These categories are discussed more fully in Cerny, "Quilted Apparel."
9. A. L. Macdonald, *No Idle Hands: The Social History of American Knitting* (New York: Ballantine Books, 1988); and Rozsika Parker, *The Subversive Stitch: Embroidery and the Making of the Feminine* (London: The Women's Press, 1986).
10. Kristin M. Langellier, "Contemporary Quiltmaking in Maine: Re-fashioning Femininity," *Uncoverings 1990*, ed. Laurel Horton (San Francisco: American Quilt Study Group, 1991), 29–55.
11. Jean Bay Wiley, "Sept. 9th Evening Meeting Report," *Minnesota Quilters News* 8 (November, 1985): 9.
12. These perspectives, similarly, characterize comments expressed by the quilters during "show-and-tell." Cerny, "Quilted Apparel," 158–181.
13. Minnesota Quilters Inc., "Scrap Quilt Magic" catalog (March 30–April 2, 1985). The 1985 "Scrap Quilt Magic" show featured eight quilts based on

the Log Cabin block. It was the most popular block of approximately 130 members' quilts on exhibit.

14. Ibid., 9. Peggy Kotek, *Bandanas*. Kotek is referring to Marguerite Ickis, *The Standard Book of Quilt Making and Collecting* (1949; repr., New York: Dover, 1959).
15. Ibid., 13. Katie Niessen, *Log Cabin—Sunshine and Shadow*.
16. Ibid., 20. Lynette Wass, *Wass' Traveling Quilt Sampler*.
17. Ibid., 3. Elizabeth Birkholz, *Log Cabin*.
18. Ibid., 5–6. Nancy Frasson, *Ken's Quilted Barn*.
19. Ibid., 20–21. Winona Area Quilters Guild, *Sampler in Blues*.
20. *Funk and Wagnalls Standard Dictionary* (New York: Signet/Lippincott and Crowell, 1980), s.v. "symbol."
21. See Sherry B. Ortner, "On Key Symbols," *American Anthropologist* 75 (September, 1973): 1339. She reviews the implications of the notion of "key symbol" in cultural analysis.
22. Ibid., 1340.
23. Langellier, 52.

Quilts Used as Backdrops in Old Photographs

Vista Anne Mahan

One hundred and ten years ago quilters were wild about the new fad of crazy quilts, and photographers were excited about new products in cameras and film. Because of the growth in the photography industry in the 1880s, we are now able to take a look at family pictures of the period, not only of the rich and famous, but of the rural and ordinary. Some of these ordinary families had their pictures made at home, on the front porch or in the front yard, using a quilt as a backdrop. Who owned these quilts? What were the conditions which led to the occasional use of quilts as backdrops in family photographs late in the nineteenth century?

The inspiration for conducting this study of old photographs which show quilts as backdrops came from two old family photos; one belongs to my family and one to my husband's family. These old photos were both made in North Georgia, but were made fifteen years and a hundred miles apart. After seeing these photographs, I was on the lookout for more quilt pictures, naively sure that I would find at least one old quilt photo in every old family photo album. Three years and many photos later, I have learned that this is not so, but with perseverance I have assembled a fascinating collection of old photographs with quilts in the background. With a few scattered exceptions, most of this collection dates from the mid-1880s to mid-1920s.

Vista Mahan is an lab instructor in Anatomy and Physiology at Chattanooga State Technical Community College. She worked as a volunteer in both the Tennessee and Georgia quilt documentation projects. She plans to continue her research on quilts in old photographs, hoping to gather photos from all areas. Route 4, Box 410, Chickamauga, GA 30707.

Changes in Photography—Style and Equipment

Beginning in the mid-1800s public appetite for photographs was immense. Technical advances in cameras and film were changing the way photographs were made.

A French artist, Louis Daguerre, gets credit for inventing the first commercially successful photographic process in 1839.[1] Within five years almost every American town of any size had a gallery where average folks could have their daguerreotypes made.[2] For the first time, people were able to purchase photographic images instead of sitting for hours while an artist painted a portrait. The photograph was an image on a silver-plated copper sheet which was placed under glass. By the mid-1840s itinerant daguerreotypists had hit the road with their cameras, developing equipment, and sheets for backdrops.[3] Exposure time ranging from many seconds or minutes varied depending on the amount of available light.

By 1851 advances in materials and technique produced a "wet-plate"—a negative on glass treated with chemicals instead of silver-plated copper. This wet-plate process allowed a shorter exposure time of a few seconds if the subject was in the sun.[4]

"People were fascinated at having their picture taken," according to Martin Sandler, a researcher of old photographs.[5] In 1857, eighteen years after the camera had been invented in France, enterprising photographers were widespread. One had already set up shop at Niagara Falls to take photos of tourists with the falls in the background.[6] By 1860, new technology had almost completely replaced the demanding daguerreotype process with the ambrotype, (an image on glass) and the tintype (actually on iron, not tin) which were easier and cheaper to produce.[7] Large scale photographic coverage of the Civil War was made possible by the advances in technique.[8] Thirty years after the invention of photography, there were enough photographers to hold a national convention in 1868.[9] Tintype photography studios were commonplace in the United States by 1871.[10]

Though improved techniques and materials continued to refine the photographic process, indoor studio exposures in the 1870s still ranged from fifteen seconds to well over a minute.[11] Subjects had to sit or stand very still for indoor pictures. But by 1878, exposures in good light shortened to a fraction of a second rather than many seconds or minutes.[12]

Before long more changes in photographic equipment and technique made photography available to the general public. In 1888, George Eastman invented and sucesssfully marketed a simple twenty-five dollar camera already loaded with film for a hundred exposures.[13] This film wasn't the bulky, messy, heavy, glass-plate variety; it was flexible film wound on a spool, "a far greater supply of material in a far more compact form."[14] The camera was simplicity itself. With no viewfinder and no focus adjustment, the camera had only to be pointed at the subject. Eastman later added some "V" sighting lines on top of the camera. A memorandum book came with the camera so details of the hundred exposures could be noted. The notes were also a reminder when the end of the roll was near.[15] When a hundred pictures were exposed, the entire camera was mailed back to Eastman's company in Rochester, New York, which developed the negatives, then mounted the prints. They mailed back the negatives, the prints, and the camera reloaded with film and charged the customer ten dollars. Eastman made up the name "Kodak" for his camera and coined a slogan to go with his new product, "You press the button, we do the rest."[16]

Now "taking pictures was so simple that no one could possibly feel it beyond his competance," and the number of amateur photographers increased astronomically. Eastman's invention and marketing of the Kodak brought the camera out of the studio.[17] The increasing number of professionals and amateurs in the late 1880s is a direct result of Eastman's introduction of paper film and roller holder.[18]

The old city directories of Chattanooga, Tennessee, document the expansion of the photographic industry in one location. The 1871–1872 city directory listed one photography gallery in town. By 1890, two years after the inventions of George Eastman, there were six galleries and two additional listings of "cameras and supplies for amateurs."

Within seven years of his inventions, Mr. Eastman saw his new products capture the American and world market. In 1895, his Rochester factory increased producion from 300 to 600 cameras a day and still couldn't meet the demand. "By the end of 1898 over 1,500,000 roll film cameras were in use throughout the world.[19] These cameras were in the hands of photographers who went about recording social history and giving us countless pictures of the "anonymous multitudes."[20]

After the 1840s, families who could afford it wanted their pictures taken. Family photos meant "that a family had leisure, clothes, and money enough—and sufficient sense of itself as an acceptable social unit—to get together, get dressed up and defy time to become part of posterity."[21] The studios or galleries in towns and cities continued to handle the growing demand for portraits.

But if the people couldn't come to the photographer, the photographer went to the people. An increasing number of itinerant photographers took to the road to cash in on the nation's craving for portraiture. They created temporary headquarters in hotels and boarding houses in county seats and large communities. After the Civil War more and more photographers adapted horse-drawn wagons for living quarters, dark rooms and studios, allowing rural settlers and small villagers to have pictures made in their own settlements or farmsteads.[22] More enterprising photographers turned railroad cars into tintype studios to park on side tracks for a few weeks until time to move on.[23] Others took pictures at camp meetings held by churches in the summer.[24] Family reunions were likely occasions for a photographer to do business. A 1918 newspaper account reports at a family reunion in Lumpkin County, Georgia, "All ate dinner and had their picture taken."[25] Some itinerants had houseboats set up as galleries to do business up and down the rivers.[26]

In the small communities the photographers announced their visits with handbills and newspaper ads and waited for the public to appear at their hotels, boarding houses, wagons, railroad cars, house boats, or studio tents. These photographers also contracted to make pictures on location at the family home.

Before the turn of the twentieth century more than half of the population of the United States made a living by farming.[27] Some photographers saw that going door to door in rural areas might yield good prospects. Struggling farm families might not get dressed up and go into town for a studio portrait, but most all could afford a picture of the family in front of the house, taken on the spot by a traveling photographer as he canvassed the countryside.[28]

Orlie Trentham became an itinerant photographer in the Smoky Mountains around 1912 or 1914 after an Army buddy taught him photography. After he made his pictures, he brought the film to his home to develop. Instead of a dark room, he had a little out building he called his "dark house." [29]

North Carolina Folklife Specialist Wayne Martin has interviewed many older rural fiddle and banjo players who have shown him photographs made by itinerant photographers. These interviews reveal that "a photographer would come to a community once or twice a year, stopping by all the farms inquiring if families wanted their picture made."[30]

The United States View Company, a Pennsylvania company which hired traveling photographers from about 1890 to 1901, produced a Policies and Procedures notebook giving detailed instructions for the photographic process. This company directed its operators to photograph family groups, farm and town houses, school groups, mills and factories, but to avoid photographing "interiors, rented houses, houses where the people will not stand out, where the people will not put on a coat or take off their hats." When a family agreed to have a picture made and went to get ready, the operator was to be setting up the photograph. "Place some chairs on the porch or in the yard to make it appear as though the family was setting [sic] out." Other instructions included, "Have all hats, bonnets and white aprons taken off, and do not have the men photographed with coats off; shirt sleeves and old clothes show bad taste to the operator." In order to have a pleasing arrangement of the group: "Never sit or stand them all in a row. Some sit, some stand. Some lean against the fence or some other suitable place. . . . Always place strangers and hired help so far to one side of the picture that they don't take." Striving for the sharpest picture, the operator was told, "Make the exposure as short as possible. Never have your hand on camera or tripod while making exposure."[31] Though no mention was made about tacking up a quilt for a backdrop, it would have been just such an occasion when a quilt might be used.

References to Photographs in Diaries and Letters

Today we see these old photos as links with the past; when they were made, the photos served as tangible connections to scattered families. Lure of land and jobs separated loved ones as children grew up and moved away from parents and siblings. Contemporary diaries and letters show how dear these photos were to faraway relatives.

The diary of Julia Stanford, a young Georgia woman, written during the Civil War, includes four references to photos during 1861. For example, on Saturday, July 27,1861, she wrote, "Frank sent me his ambrotype, also a letter, both of which I prize highly." Thirty years later, Julia's niece Mattie Dillard kept a diary from 1887 to 1891, and three times she mentions exchanging photos with friends.[32]

Another Georgia family prizes the photographs which were mentioned in letters written from 1896 to 1915 by branches of the family who had left Georgia to go west to Missouri and Arkansas. On February 9,1896, a grown daughter, Martha Glaze Brownlow, wrote from Arkansas to her parents, Willis and Martha Glaze, back in Mossy Creek, Georgia. "I wish I could see you all. I wont you all to hurry and send me your pictures. You just don't no how bad I want to see them. . . . I wont you all every one of you to send me your pictures. Martha B to Pa and Mother." Seven months later Martha received pictures in the mail. One picture was to be given to a relative who was staying nearby with a sick neighbor. After promptly delivering the picture to the relative, Martha wrote to her parents. "I received your letter and pictures last night . . . I took hur picture to hur this morning and she said she woulden sleep any for a week now. She would haf to look at them all the time."

In August 1899, Martha wrote, "Tell all the children that has there pictures taken at Camp M. to send me one—children and grandchildren. If you and Pa have your pictures taken at Camp Meeting you send me one and tell John to send me one of his to." So a photographer must have seen the possibilities of taking pictures at a church camp meeting.

After sending a photo to a relative in Missouri, Willis and Martha Glaze received this response, dated August 29, 1897. "We can't tell you how glad we all was to git your picture. Willis is like his father and Martha must be awful fleshy and Molly thinks that John is a pretty boy. You all must have plenty to eat there. Tell all the children we would like to git all of ther pictures."[33]

Poses and Props

Photographers and most of the families they photographed had seen photographs of the famous, the wealthy, and of course, other ordinary families. No doubt the photographers were aware of trends of their trade—which poses sold better, which studio props made a picture more interesting, which prized family possessions worked well in a picture.

During the early years of photography a plain backdrop was the most desirable. During the 1850s, canvas backdrops painted with classical scenes or scenes from nature were favored.[34] One description of a fancy studio in New York City in 1870 states, "He has more than fifty painted backgrounds representing sea and sky, plains and mountains, tropic luxuriance and polar wastes; every style of scenery from Egypt to Siberia." This collection "grew to 150 backgrounds, until his studio looked like the property room of an enormous theatre."[35]

Even more modest galleries would have some kind of painted backgrounds and accessories: "imitation stone often covered with paper ivy, an uprooted tree, the parchment rocks." Styles changed and "a castle or two, mock furniture (piano), the boats, and the sleighs in endless profusion" became favorites.[36] By the beginning of the Civil War one studio photograph looked like most any other studio photograph—a "full-length figure standing beside a column, with other accessories thrown in for good measure, depending on the operator's taste, or lack of it."[37]

While studio photographs were enhanced with fancy settings and props, the traveling photographer was limited to what he could carry or find on location. Due to poor indoor lighting, the traveling photographer "liked to capture his subjects on the front porch—where the lighting was much better."[38] While setting up the picture, the photographer might ask the family if they had any prized possessions to be included in the photograph. Such portraits captured the character, as well as the likeness, of the family.[39] They show what people were proud of, thought interesting, and what they wanted to show others.[40]

Some of the most intriguing home portraits picture the family in front of a quilt. Given the elaborate backdrops of some studios, perhaps it is not surprising that during the last quarter of the nineteenth century photographers occasionally used family quilts as a backdrop on the front porch and also in the yard. This was a practical way to make the subjects stand out from their background. Because many homes were constructed of unpainted bare wood siding, a quilt substituted as a canvas backdrop for the itinerants with little or no operating budgets. The family itself took pride in using a quilt that was important to them.[41] Some people used woven coverlets or other textiles as backdrops, and a few even used rugs or carpets.[42] According to one country photographer, "We find that fancy backgrounds and appropriate accessories are the things necessary for a continued revival of trade."[43]

Description of Quilt Photographs

I have collected eighty-five photographs which feature quilts used as backdrops. I also noted related photos. Though woven coverlets were not the focus of my research, I found I could not pass up these textile backdrops whenever I came across them. I have nineteen examples showing woven coverlets. In addition there were eleven "mystery" textile backdrops, probably rugs, carpets, bedspreads, or tablecloths.

The photographs came from many sources. I searched through thousands of old photographs in state archive collections—Georgia, Tennessee, Alabama, and Arkansas. Georgia and Tennessee have excellent old photograph collections acquired in much the same way many states conducted quilt documentation projects. With advance publicity, teams from the state archives went to different areas of the state and set up photography equipment to copy old photographs brought to the site by the general public. When available, background information was recorded about each photograph copied. None of the archive collections were indexed according to the presence or absence of quilts, so I looked at an unbelievable number of pictures of politicians, street scenes, railroad and mill work, natural disasters, and ordinary families without quilts as backdrops! I looked at 8,000 to 10,000 old photographs in the Tennessee State Library and Archives alone.

Other sources of my quilt photographs include fellow American Quilt Study Group members who learned of my research through the newsletter *Blanket Statements* and then sent me their own old family photos or photos they had purchased from antique dealers or flea markets. I located some photographs through several museum, college, and historical society archive collections. Some came from pictorial county history books. Interestingly, I found no quilt backdrop photographs in the collections of the National Archives, Smithsonian Photographic Archives, D.A.R.Museum, George Eastman International Museum of Photography, nor the Library of Congress Prints and Photographs Division.

Dates of the Quilt Photographs

Some of the photographs had dates written on the back, most likely put there by family members. Other dates were derived from the people identified in the photograph, for instance from the date of birth of a baby, date of death, or marriage date. An 1860 family picture of my great-great-grandparents, Emily and Francis Marion Crumly and their young son and daughter, is the oldest photo in this collection. The date of the photograph is based upon the date of death of little John Henry Crumly. Approximate dates of other pictures have been assigned after study of costumes by a museum textile and costume curator. Some have remained undated because of lack of significant details in the photographs. Some photos were produced to be used as postcards and consequently have a postmark. Other photographic postcards were dated by the styles of typeface on the printed labels which framed the area for placement of the postage stamp or the area of the address.[44]

The quilts themselves were not used to date the photographs. The families could have chosen old family quilts as backdrops just for sentimental reasons. Or a new quilt may have been proudly displayed, a symbol of the family's ability to keep up with recent trends of fashionable needlework. Therefore an approximate date of a photograph indicates only that the quilt was already made at that time, and the quilt could, of course, be much older than the photograph.

Methods of Hanging a Quilt Backdrop

The method of hanging the quilt for the backdrop showed several variations. While the top of the quilt was cropped out of some pictures, other photos plainly showed the top of the quilt to be tacked with nails to the side of the house or some outbuilding. One photo shows the quilt wedged between chinks in a log structure. Clotheslines supported some quilts. Children are sometimes posed in a chair draped with a quilt across the back of the chair. In many of the photos grass or dirt can be seen at the feet, and in others the foundation of the house is visible. All but one or two of the pictures were made outdoors.

Quilt Patterns

THE CRAZY QUILT

The single most common type of quilt to show up as a backdrop in the family photographs in my collection was the crazy quilt—seventeen out of eighty-five. Ten crazy quilt photos have approximate dates, the earliest circa 1890 and the latest 1920. Of these ten photos seven date from the decade 1890–1900. These photos fall

Figure 1. The Joseph Silbernagel family hung two quilts for a backdrop in this 1910 or 1911 photograph. Joseph was born in Russia, emigrated to North Dakota ca. 1900, and moved on to Alberta, Canada, in 1908. Courtesy of Glenbow Archives, Calgary, Canada, photo # NA-4079–44.

right in the middle peak popularity years for crazy quilts, 1880 to 1910.[45]

One of the crazy quilt photos shows the fourteen well-dressed Silbernagels, an immigrant family, posed in front of a large expanse of utilitarian crazy patches enhanced with some feather stitch embroidery (Figure 1). The backdrop is probably two quilts hung side by side; what appears to be the bound edge of one quilt is centered in the photo. The head of the family is recorded as Joseph Silbernagel, who was born in Russia, emigrated to North Dakota, and later moved on to Alberta, Canada, where this picture was made in 1910 or 1911.

Throughout the collection of old photographs, the facial expressions of almost all the people are solemn. In 1899, a photographer captured the stern face and posture of Nan Ross in her rick-rack embellished blouse. Nan, her two sisters Mattie and Sue, and their

Figure 2. Nan Ross stands in front of a Crazy Quilt, commenced in February and finished in December of 1898. Nan, Mattie, Sue and their mother Elizabeth Charles Ross made the quilt. It has the initials of all twelve children and the marriage date of Tom Ross and Elizabeth Charles. Courtesy of Tennessee State Library and Archives, Looking Back at Tennessee Collection.

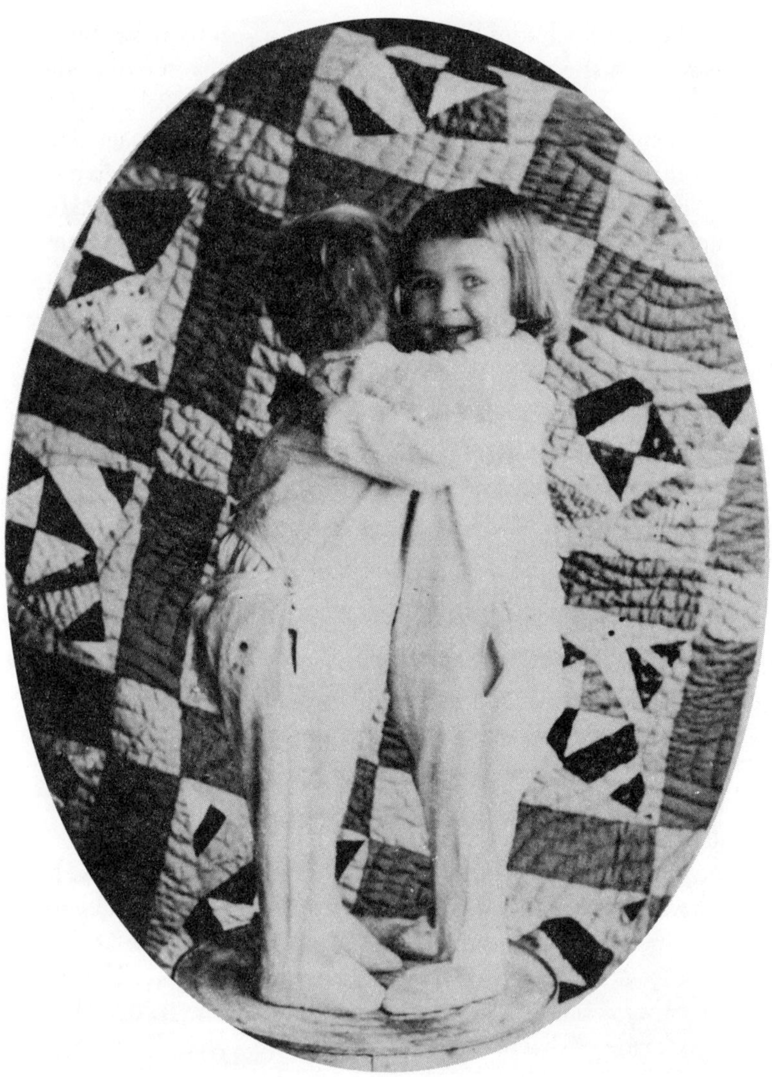

Figure 3. In Fayetteville, Georgia, twins John and Mildred Stell stood on an overturned washtub for their photograph in 1907. The Rocky Road to Kansas quilt was made by Talula Bottoms. Courtesy of Nancilu Burdick. Photo previously published in *Family Ties: Old Quilt Patterns from New Cloth*, Rutledge Hill Press,1991.

mother Elizabeth Charles Ross took most of a year to make the crazy quilt shown in the photograph (Figure 2). They even embroidered the beginning and ending date on the quilt, "Comm. Feb. 1898 Finished December 1898." The quilt also includes the marriage date of Tom and Elizabeth Charles and the initials of all their twelve children. The photograph was made in Hawkins County, Tennessee.[46]

Happier expressions are found on the faces of two Tennessee couples, the Hedgecoths and the Hambys, in front of another crazy quilt. The two infants in the photograph, born nine days apart in 1912, grew up and later married each other.[47]

The crazy quilts in the photographs reflect a range of fabrics and amount of embellishment. Ten of the seventeen quilts pictured appear to have velvets, satins, brocades, and an array of fancy embroidery stitches covering every seam. The other seven are utilitarian crazy quilts, made from wool or cotton dress and shirting scraps, with simple embroidery around some of the pieces.

LOG CABIN AND ROCKY ROAD TO KANSAS

Log Cabin and Rocky Road to Kansas are tied for second most frequently found pattern amoung quilt backdrops, each occurring in five photos. These patterns can be made up in fancy fabrics or in the scraps left over from sewing family clothes. Regardless, both the Log Cabin and Rocky Road to Kansas achieve the scrap look so popular in the late nineteenth century.[48]

One of the sweetest pictures shows young twins, Mildred and John Stell, standing on an overturned wash tub in front of a Rocky Road to Kansas quilt made by their aunt Talula Bottoms (Figure 3). Talula made the quilt for her half-sister Betty, the twins' mother. The twins' older brother, Hugh Stell, took the photograph in 1907. He had postcards made of this picture and sent one to Talula.[49]

One of the first two quilt photos I found was of my great-aunt's family in front of a Rocky Road to Kansas quilt (Figure 4). Alice Carrie Belle Jarrard Beach sits with her husband Ed and three unhappy children, all looking sternly at the photographer. The photograph was probably set up in their front yard in the mountains of Georgia, ca. 1915.

One of the five log cabin quilt photos shows the Satterfields of

Figure 4. The author's great-aunt Carrie Belle Jarard Beach, her husband Ed, and three children, Henry, Ethleen, and James, posed in front of an unquilted Rocky Road to Kansas, ca. 1915. The major pieces of the quilt design are outlined in feather stitch embroidery typical of fancy stitches on crazy quilts of that era. Photograph, collection of the author.

White County, Georgia, in front of two quilts—a log cabin and a four-pointed star.[50]

STRING QUILTS AND DOUBLE-T

The next most frequent types of quilt to appear are three string quilts and three T-quilts. Along with crazy quilts and log cabin quilts, the string quilts are a type of foundation patchwork. This technique utilized a piece of fabric or paper cut to a given size. Then other smaller fabrics were sewn piece by piece over the foundation until it was covered. Since these three foundation types are featured so often in this collection of quilt photos, it confirms that foundation patchwork was widespread in the last quarter of the nineteenth century. Foundation patchwork maintained its popularity for years. Even after the making of crazy quilts peaked from 1880 to 1910, string quilts continued to be common from 1890 to 1940.[51]

Around 1890, four generations of the Howard family hung a string quilt on the porch of their Tennessee log house and gathered around "Granny" Howard to have their picture made. The six somber Howards are all well-dressed; the women are wearing pretty jewelry on their high-neck dresses and the men are in three-piece suits. Granny is holding a book—likely the family Bible. The quilt appears to be unquilted.

Another Tennessee family, the Youngs, tacked up a utilitarian string quilt on the side of their home in 1900. Mother, father, two daughters, and the family dog stand in front of the quilt. The quilting was done in a fan pattern.

MIXED PATTERNS

Three photos make up a category showing quilts completed with a combination of at least two different pieced block patterns. The quiltmakers could have intended the quilts to be utility quilts from the beginning and therefore were not concerned with a few mismatched blocks. Alternatively, the quiltmakers may have run out of a particular fabric and used unmatched blocks to make the quilt longer or wider. In one of these three photos, a 1924 Georgia example, two women holding their babies posed in front of a quilt made predominantly of the Fish Tail pattern with a few Nine Patch blocks thrown in. Lelar Thompson was holding George, and Eula Coleman was holding Vilena. The quilt was wedged between the logs of the structure to secure it as a backdrop.

OTHER PATTERNS

Of the eighty-five quilt photos, two quilts are Star of LeMoyne. In 1910 the Farmer family of Tennessee dressed up to have their picture made in front of their Star of LeMoyne quilt. The two little boys are in suits with knee length pants. The quilt features star blocks alternating with plain blocks and is quilted in an overall fan or elbow pattern.

A 1920 Arkansas photo features Sarah Ellen Seay Hall seated in front of a Star of LeMoyne. The quilting is composed of diagonal

Figure 5. Andrew Jackson Daniel and Josephine Daniel Armour sat in front of a Seven Sisters quilt in the late 1880s or early 1890s. Union Parish, Louisiana. Courtesy of Sandra Todaro.

lines in the center and fan quilting in the border. Sarah Ellen was born in 1843 and married in 1860. Her husband was a Confederate soldier in the Civil War. She was seventy-six years old at the time this photo was made. Her descendants say that Sarah Ellen was an "excellent seamstress and thought to have made quilts." The photographer, who posed Sarah Ellen with the romance stories she loved to read, was her granddaughter Mabel Hall Smith.[52]

Two photos with Lone Star quilts are represented in this study. A young Tennessean, Clarence Stephens, stands in front of a Lone Star, nicely quilted in a grid pattern in the plain areas and with outline quilting in the diamonds of the large star. This is the only photograph I found with an exact month, day, and year—August 30, 1904.[53]

The Seven Sisters pattern shows up in two photos, both made in the south. In a Louisiana photo, Andrew Jackson Daniel and his sister Josephine Daniel Armour sat to have their picture made (Figure 5). Josephine is dressed in mourning clothes. The Seven Sisters quilt is assembled without sashing and is quilted in concentric circles around the field of stars and diagonal lines in the border. Sandra Todaro, the great-great-granddaughter of Andrew Daniel, does not know the fate of the quilt, which would now be about one hundred years old.[54]

In an Alabama photo, the Thomas family gathered for a portrait in their front yard on a winter's day. Several features of this 1898 photo make it unusual. The fourteen people had possessions they wanted included in the photo—two guns, a banjo, a horse, some fabrics on bare tree branches, and four quilts on the porch rail: a Tree of Life variation, a Snail Trail, a Seven Sisters, and a Wild Goose Chase. Mary Ann Rouse Thomas, the maker of the four quilts, is wearing an apron. Her great-grandson, Robert Cargo, says that three of the four quilts have survived to the present. He has the Seven Sisters quilt which is put together with sashing and cornerstones. The Snail Trail quilt on the porch rail shows up as a backdrop in another family photograph, one of James William Thomas holding a banjo. Today this Snail Trail quilt belongs to a granddaughter of the quilt maker.[55]

Two photographs depict variations of the Fish Tail (or Lazy Daisy).

Figure 6. An unidentified couple posed in front of a North Carolina Lily quilt, ca. 1890. Fan quilting is visible on the quilt. Perhaps this was a wedding photograph. Courtesy of Tennessee State Museum.

Other pieced quilt patterns are represented in only one photograph: Streak of Lightning, Nine Patch, Irish Chain, London Roads variation, North Carolina Lily (Figure 6), Young Man's Fancy, Pin Wheel, Gordian Knot, Texas Star, Wild Goose Chase variation, and Shoo Fly.

Five photos show quilts made up of plain squares, rectangles, or bars. In an undated photograph, an unidentified black family posed in front of a quilt made of bars, quilted in a fan pattern.

Eight photos appear to feature either whole cloth quilts or just the plain backing of the quilt. In a 1910 photo, little Hazel Brown gathered her favorite toys and her doll and stood beside her little chair for a picture in front of a quilt, either the back of a quilt or a plain whole cloth quilt.

In this collection of eighty-five old photos, only one photo shows an appliqued quilt. Perhaps any special efforts women made on quilts during this time went toward construction of elaborate crazy quilts, and not applique quilts. However this does not explain why older applique quilts belonging to the family were not chosen as a backdrop. Perhaps families valued them too much to nail them on the wall. The absence of applique quilts during this time period was also noted by at least one state quilt documentation team: "Few applique quilts made between 1890 and 1920 came to North Carolina documentation days."[56]

Quilting Designs

About half of the eighty-five photographs have images which are clear enough to see the design of the quilting itself. The most frequently occurring quilting design is the fan, also known as the elbow or shell. The concentric arcs of the fan are visible in eighteen quilts. Fan quilting was a fast, practical way to get a quilt top done. It was suited to group work or individual quilting, and was common for quilts made after 1875.[57]

Fan quilting can be seen on a quilt hanging behind Callie Davenport and her son in a ca. 1910 photo. The quilt may be a whole cloth quilt of fabric printed to look like pieced blocks. The concentric arcs are a prominent feature of another quilt behind an unidentified man (Figure 7). The quilt is a variation of Stepping Stones or Rocky Road to California. Fan quilting is also featured on a North Carolina Lily quilt. The unidentified well-dressed young couple are perhaps posing for a wedding picture.

Ten quilts were quilted in an all-over design: straight line diagonal row, cross hatch, or clam shell. The trend during 1891 to 1920 was for less elaborate quilting. Quilts were regarded as functional bedding for rural middle and lower classes—the very people featured in many photos in this collection.[58] Two additional photos clearly show an outline stitch around the pieced quilt blocks.

Eleven families hung unquilted tops or summer spreads for their portraits. A quilt top, rather than a finished quilt, might show a woman's most recent efforts. The new top might have been considered a nicer choice for a backdrop than the well-worn quilts in constant use on the beds. The lighter weight quilt tops also would have been easier to tack up on a wall than heavier three-layered finished quilts.

The first two quilt photos which formed the inspiration for this research project feature unquilted quilts. My husband's great-great-grandparents Lecil and Lemilia Day sit in front of a Broken Dishes quilt top. The photo was made in Northwest Georgia between 1900–1915. No one knows if the quilt still exists today. The other photo is my great-aunt's family in front of an unquilted Rocky Road to Kansas. With embroidery along the seam lines, the quilt is reminicent of the crazy quilt style which would usually remain unquilted. Another unquilted Rocky Road to Kansas is the backdrop in an undated and unidentified Tennessee photo.

Three of the eighty-five photographs illustrate tied quilts. Tying or tacking was a quick way to produce covers for warmth. Tying a quilt was especially popular from 1880 to the 1930s.[59] In an undated photo from the Smoky Mountain area, an attractive, well-dressed couple, Sherman and Alice Myers, are shown in front of a tied quilt. The yard looks as if it might have a little snow on it.[60]

The eleven unquilted tops, plus the seventeen crazy quilts, and the three tied quilts make up thirty-one of the eighty-five photographs; therefore, thirty-six percent of the collection are unquilted.

Figure 7. Unidentified man, undated. The quilt is a variation of Stepping Stones, finished with fan quilting. Photo purchased at a farm auction in Cannon County, Tennessee. Courtesy of Thelma Hibdon and Folk Arts Program/ Tennessee Arts Commission.

A possible reason for the selection of a crazy quilt or an unquilted top could have been the desire to use the newest quilt in the house. A crazy quilt would have indicated the family's ability to keep up to date with trends in home furnishings, decorating the parlor with this embroidered piece work. Quilting designs were not discernible for the remaining twenty-five quilt photographs in this collection.

Posing the People for Their Portraits

Twenty-four photographs show more than just people in front of a quilt. Onto the porch or yard came an interesting array of possessions. Some families brought out the new parlor organ or the sewing machine. Others displayed family heirlooms such as portraits or Bibles.[61] Books became a "standard prop to symbolize literacy." People wanted to record those material possessions which were dear to them—guns, knives, rocking chairs, quilts, coverlets, banjos, fiddles, horses, pets, and dolls.[62] Perhaps having seen studio portraits made with various props, the itinerant photographer wanted to make his or her pictures more like the studio versions by including possessions or pets. The families themselves may have wanted to be photographed with favorite or important possessions. "It was a common practice in our Smokies area to be photographed with a 'prized possession'. . . guns, knives, dogs, horses, musical instruments, Bibles," according to local historian Gladys T. Russell.[63] In five photographs, women are holding flowers. Various pets, such as dogs and a cat, were included in four photos. Little Gordon Shannon sat on a rocking chair holding his pet chicken. The quilt is a Triple Irish Chain pieced with unusually large squares in this Tennessee photo from ca. 1915. In a 1906 picture, the Climer family of nine adults, two babies, and a little black dog assembled in front of a Gordian Knot quilt.

Five photos feature musical instruments, banjos and one accordion. Guns or knives appear in three photos. Three young East Tennessee mountain men stand in front of a utilitarian quilt sometime between 1918 and 1922. One holds a gun, one has a banjo, and one holds a gun and a knife. The picture has an air of comedy for us looking at it seventy years later. A Streak of Lightning quilt is the backdrop for Spencer Gosnell of Sodom, North Carolina. This ca. 1910 photo shows Spencer with a gun in each hand.[64] Four photos show persons holding books.

Even dead babies and adults were sometimes photographed. "To obtain an acccurate visual record of their loved ones, family members commissioned these memorial portraits, which were also taken of those who died in middle or old age."[65] A sad photo taken in Tennessee in the first decade of this century is evidence of this practice. This was the only picture of all three Likens children, Tommy and Nora, with their dead baby sister Donna.

Multi-Quilt Backdrops

Most of the poses in the photographs I collected involved arranging the families in front of only one quilt. In six photographs it took two quilts to cover the expanse. A two-quilt backdrop was used for the Silvers family. The back of the photo had this bit of information, "Members of John Wesley Silvers family dressed in their Sunday finery pose for this group portrait. Perhaps the watermelon at the left was to be eaten after the photograph had been taken." This photograph was made in Georgia around 1900. The two quilts don't seem to be as elaborate as the Sunday clothes. One quilt appears to have plain blocks put together with sashing. The other quilt is either a whole cloth quilt or the back of a quilt. Both are fan quilted.

In 1910 the Rupper family of Tennessee hung two quilt tops on a line and had their picture made in front of them. One top is a Double-T and the other is Triangles. The seated matron is holding flowers.[66]

Sometimes it took more than two quilts to make the picture complete,as with the aforementioned Thomas family photograph made in Alabama in 1898 which featured four quilts on the porch rail. There is a nine-quilt photograph made about the same time in Georgia. The Holloway family hung nine quilts on the fence in front of the house for their family portrait (Figure 8). There's no explanation for why so many quilts were included. The family may have been especially proud of the collection of good quilts they owned

Figure 8. In the late 1800s, the Holloway family of Sumter County, Georgia, stood for a group picture by the front fence covered with nine quilts. (Hint: there are two quilts on the open gate.) Courtesy of Georgia Department of Archives and History.

and wanted them in the picture. Or perhaps the photographer came along on a nice day when the quilts were being aired out. Perhaps these quilts were being displayed on the fence because they were for sale. The nine quilts are identified from left to right: Twelve Triangles, variation of Wild Goose Chase-Rocky Mountain Road combination, Pinwheel, two more of the same combinations of Wild Goose Chase-Rocky Mountain Road, two unidentified quilts on the open gate, Double-T, and Pickle Dish.[67]

Conclusions

The scattered occurences of quilt backdrop photographs over a wide geographic area document that this practice was popular in the southeastern United States, and perhaps in other areas as well. The states where the quilt photographs in this collection were made were Georgia, Tennessee, Arkansas, North Carolina, Alabama, Kentucky, Louisiana, and Virginia. However, there were many photographs found which had no information available. The discovery of the Canadian photo of the Silbernagel family suggests that this type of picture may have been made throughout the United States, wherever itinerant photographers traveled house to house. As more research is done, I believe photographs from other areas of the United States will be identified by quilt researchers, quilt lovers, and photograph collectors.

Who owned the quilts—the family or the photographer? The evidence gathered would support the theory that the quilts belonged to the family being photographed and not to the itinerant photographer. Some people living today were able to tell some details about itinerant photography. John R. Cofield, born February 8, 1918, showed me a 1927 family picture with his mother's woven wool "coverlid" as a backdrop. He told me about his photograph and described how a photographer worked the rural area of Randolph County, Alabama.

> We had traveling photographers (horse and buggy) who came through our area every summer. Made pictures on credit, could pay when the cotton was sold in the fall if short on cash then. I don't think the man

> carried backdrops; they were furnished by the household. Some people used rugs (carpets) for backgrounds. My parents had twelve postcard size photographs made of . . . the children. Mother wove this [backdrop coverlid] on a loom (large type). It was made of wool from sheep pastured on her mother's farm. . . . My grandmother kept three black sheep for black wool.[68]

Connie Burkhalter, a staff photographer with the photography project, Looking Back at Tennessee, at the Tennessee State Library and Archives writes,

> I do know that it was a common practice that the items photographed in these portraits were prized possessions of the owners. The quilts were most often family heirlooms or made by someone in the portrait. However, we know some quilts were just pretty backgrounds. During our travels working on the Looking Back at Tennessee project, I talked with family members who still owned a quilt which was used in an old photograph.[69]

There are other documented cases where the source of the backdrop is known. Setha Jane Stele wove a coverlet which was used as a backdrop in a 1908 photo. The loom she used to make the coverlet was later donated to Berry College. Then in 1914, Setha Jane made a crazy quilt which was used as a backdrop when her two sons posed for a portrait in 1920.[70] The crazy quilt hanging behind the stern-looking Nan Ross was made by Nan and her two sisters and mother in 1898.

Mrs. Marcelle Coker White, a fourth generation quiltmaker, tells about a 1908 photograph of her great-grandmother, Louisa Rogers Elrod (Figure 9). Louisa's daughters Josie, age fifteen, and Ida, age thirteen, are standing beside their mother. The three of them are standing in front of a quilt Louisa made. The family calls the quilt "Young Man's Fantasy." A few years ago, this old photograph inspired Louisa's granddaughter Hope Bramblett Wood to duplicate the quilt, since no one knew what became of the original. Hope did not have a pattern for the quilt and had difficulty trying to draft the block in the correct proportions. She said that one night a voice spoke to her in a dream, "Honey, if you will cut the piece in the middle just like the one on the side it will work O.K." Hope tried it the next morning, and "it went together like a charm."[71]

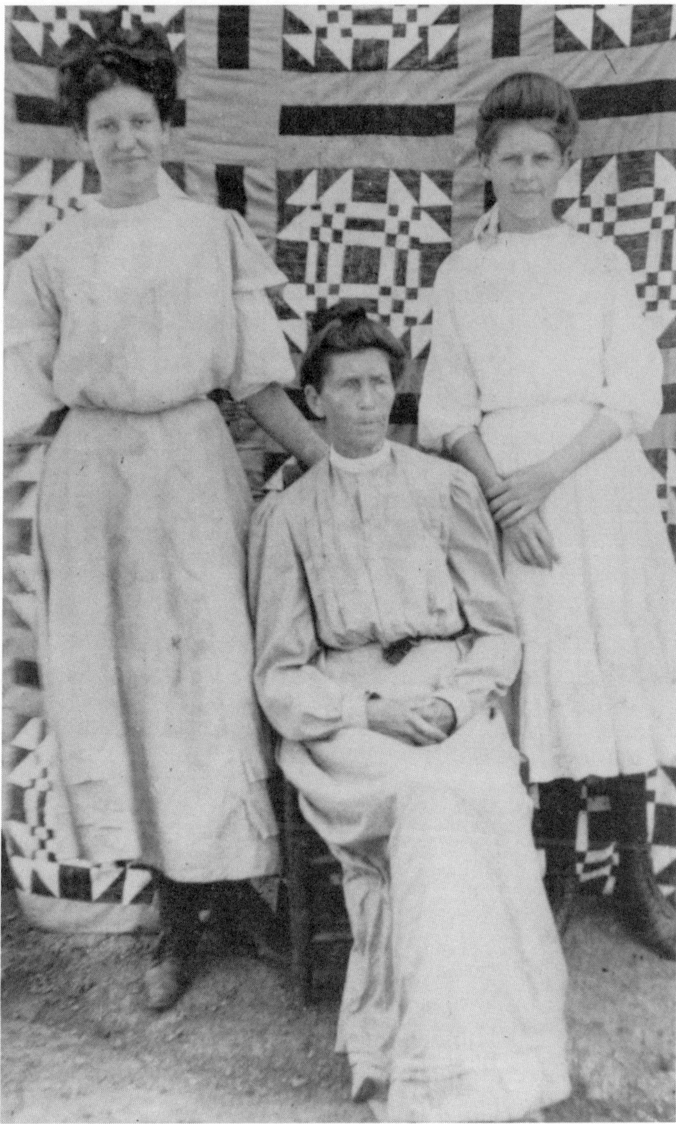

Figure 9. Jessie Josephine "Josie" Elrod (age fifteen), Louisa Rogers Elrod, and Ida Estelle Elrod (age thirteen) pose ca. 1908 in front of a quilt Louisa made. The family calls this quilt "Young Man's Fantasy." Murray County, Georgia. Courtesy of Marcelle Coker White.

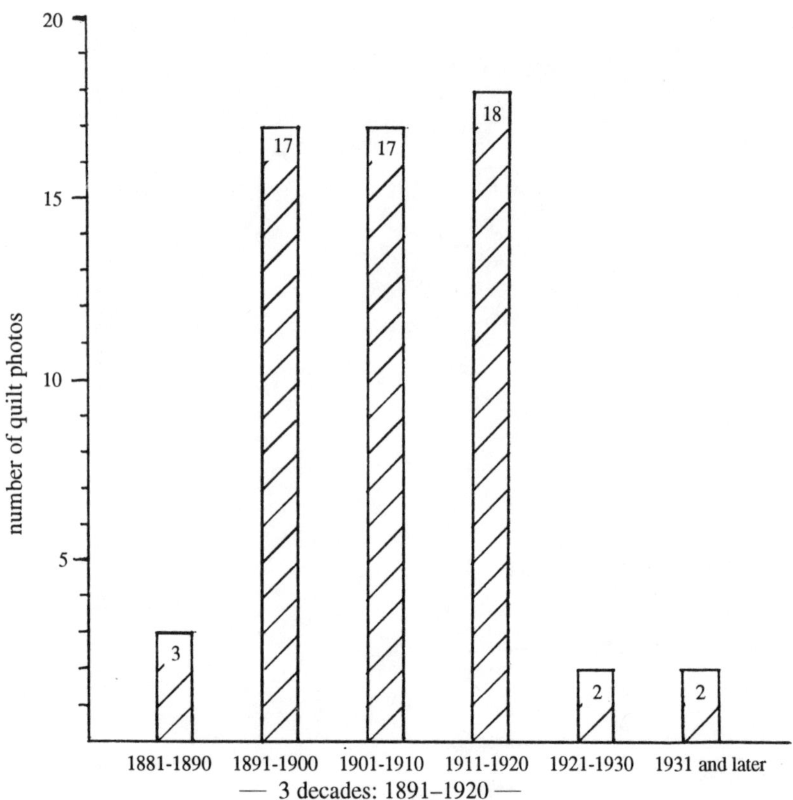

Figure 10. Of the 59 photographs in my collection for which dates can be attributed, the great majority were taken in the three decade period 1891–1920.

My research indicates that the use of quilts as backdrops for photography occurred primarily through three decades from 1891 to 1920. (See Figure 10) The information gathered from these photographs adds evidence to the body of knowledge about quiltmaking in that time period. Old quilt photos confirm trends that quilt historians have noted for those years—the popularity of the crazy quilt, log cabin, and string quilts and the basic fan quilting pattern. Near the end of those years, a new style of quilt became popular. The pretty pastel prints of the Depression era and the new quilt patterns of Dresden Plate, Double Wedding Ring, and Dutch Doll (Sunbonnet Sue) took over the quilt world, but are conspicuously absent in my study. No butterflies outlined in black embroidery can be found as backdrops. Likewise the yo-yo and pastel Grandmother's Flower Garden are absent. By the time these new quilt trends were widespread, the heyday of the itinerant photographer was over.

By the end of these three decades rural lifestyles and traveling photographers had given way to urban jobs and family ownership of cameras. Door-to-door photographers, as well as the families they photographed, no longer traveled in horse-drawn buggies but in automobiles. Some photographers even took to airplanes for aerial views.[72] Posing the pictures on the front porch vanished along with the job description of the itinerant photographer. More and more families acquired cameras, and a typical family could easily pose in front of its newest, most impressive possession—the family automobile.

Additional work by costume experts to date some of the photos will help to analyze the data. Just as it is important to sign and date a quilt, it is essential that photographs be identified with names, dates, and locations.

A larger number of old photographs could tell us about regional variation in the number of quilt photos produced and can give us a more definitive beginning and ending date for the practice of using quilts as backdrops. Surveying larger numbers of old quilt photos will add a new dimension to quilt history, thereby telling us more about quilts and their uses in old photographs. By working together, quilt researchers, photo collectors, and textile historians can collaborate to provide details on this significant but rarely mentioned practice within portrait photography, which will ultimately better our understanding of American life at the turn of the twentieth century.

Acknowledgments

I wish to thank the sources and the lenders of these photographs who have made my research a delight to conduct. Alabama Department of Archives and History; Arkansas History Commission; East Tennessee State University, Archives of Appalachia; Georgia Department of Archives and History, "Vanishing Georgia"; Georgia Quilt Project; Mars Hill College, Southern Appalachian Photographic Archives; Memphis State University, "Mississippi Valley Collection"; Tennessee Arts Commission; Tennessee State Library and Archives, "Looking Back at Tennessee"; Tennessee State Museum; Glenbow Archives, Calgary, Canada; Cuesta Benberry; Barbara Brackman; Nancilu Burdick; Robert Cargo; Frank and Callie Caruthers; John R. Cofield; Dorothy Cozart; Billie Crumly; Annie Ruth Davis; Barbara Elwell; Barbara Green Graham; Frank Green; Marybelle Hall; Thelma Hibdon; Jonathan Holstein; Doris Hoover; Laurel Horton; Mary K. Jones; Mary Kinser; Bob and Hollan Mahan; Charles Mahan; Jim Mahan; Rion Mahan; Johnny and Joy Mahan; Ruth Montgomery; Bets Ramsey; Marilyn Rogers; Gladys T. Russell; Sandra Todaro; Merikay Waldvogel; Marcelle Coker White. I also wish to thank the many friends and relatives who looked through countless photographs hunting for a quilt backdrop and didn't find one.

Notes and References

1. Linda Joan Smith, "Daguerreotypes: Intimate Reflections of Another Age," *Country Home* (Febuary 1989): 50.
2. Ibid., 108.
3. Ibid.
4. Oliver Jensen, Joan Paterson Kerr, and Murray Belsky, *American Album* (n.p.: American Heritage Publishing Co., 1968), 18.
5. Martin W. Sandler, *The Way We Lived: A Photographic Record of Work in a Vanished America* (Boston: Little, Brown & Co., 1977), vi.
6. William Welling, *Photography in America: The Formative Years 1839–1900* (New York: Thomas Y. Crowell, 1978), 127.
7. Smith, 108.
8. Welling, 163.
9. Ibid., 195.
10. Ibid., 213.
11. Robert Taft, *Photography and the American Scene* (New York: Macmillian, 1938; repr., New York: Dover, 1964), 347.
12. Brian Coe and Paul Gates, *The Snapshot Photograph: The Rise of Popular Photography 1888–1939* (London: Ash and Grant, 1977), 16.
13. Peter Pollack, *The Picture History of Photography* (New York: Harry N. Abrams, 1969), 236.
14. Taft, 384.

15. Coe and Gates, 16.
16. Pollack, 236.
17. Jean-Luc Daval, *Photography* (New York: Rizzoli International Publications, 1982), 104.
18. Taft, 386.
19. Coe and Gates, 19,21.
20. Jensen, 14.
21. Jeffrey Simpson, *The American Family: A History in Photographs* (New York: Viking Press, 1976), 11.
22. Jay Ruby, "Photographic View Companies: The Camera Leaves the Studio," *Pennsylvania Heritage* (Fall 1984): 26–31.
23. Nancilu Burdick, letter to author, July 6, 1991.
24. Martha Glaze Brownlow, letter to Willis and Martha Glaze, August 17, 1899. Collection of the author. Willis and Martha Glaze are the author's great-great-grandparents.
25. Andrew Cain, *History of Lumpkin County 1832–932* (Atlanta: Stein Printing Co., 1932), 388.
26. Warren Brunner, letter to author, June 17, 1991.
27. Simpson, 11.
28. George Talbot, *At Home: Domestic Life in the Post Centennial Era 1876–1920* (Milwaukee: Frank R. Wilke Co., 1976), vi.
29. Gladys T. Russell, letter to author, June 17, 1991.
30. Wayne Martin, letter, June 19, 1991.
31. Ruby, 26–31.
32. Diaries of Mattie Dillard, the great-grandmother of Charles Mahan, and Mattie's aunt, Julia Stanford. Copies of diaries in collection of Charles Mahan, author's husband.
33. Author's collection of old family letters of Willis and Martha Glaze, Martha Glaze Brownlow, and other unidentified relatives.
34. Ross Kelbaugh, letter, August 11, 1991. Kelbaugh is the author of *Civil War Photography*.
35. Taft, 351.
36. Taft, 335.
37. Taft, 321.
38. Jensen, 205.
39. Kelbaugh letter.
40. Talbot, iv.
41. Kelbaugh letter.
42. John R. Cofield, letter, October 17, 1988.
43. Taft, 354.

44. Hal Morgan and Andreas Brown, *Prarie Fires and Paper Moons: The American Photographic Postcard 1900–1920* (Boston: D.R. Godine, 1981), Appendix 187–190.
45. Barbara Brackman, *Clues in the Calico: A Guide to Identifying and Dating Antique Quilts* (Alexandria, Virginia: EPM, 1989), 145.
46. "Looking Back at Tennessee," Tennessee State Library and Archives.
47. Ibid.
48. Ruth Haislip Roberson, ed., *North Carolina Quilts* (Chapel Hill: University of North Carolina Press, 1988), 19.
49. Burdick letter.
50. White County History Book Committee, *A History of White County [Georgia] 1857–1980* (n.p., n.d.).
51. Brackman, 99, 145.
52. Marybelle Hall, letter to author, January 9, 1989.
53. "Looking Back at Tennessee."
54. Sandra Todaro, letter to author, July 6, 1991.
55. Robert Cargo, telephone conversation with author, June 25,1991.
56. Roberson, 19.
57. Brackman, 116.
58. Brackman, 25,26.
59. Brackman, 117.
60. Gladys T. Russell, *Smoky Mountain Family Album* (Alcoa, Tennessee: Russell Publishing Co., 1984), 308.
61. Talbot, 41.
62. Kelbaugh, letter.
63. Russell letter.
64. Southern Appalachian Photographic Archives, Mars Hill College.
65. Smith, 50. Also Gail Andrews Trechsel, "Mourning Quilts in America," *Uncoverings 1989*, ed. Laurel Horton, (San Francisco: American Quilt Study Group, 1990), 139–58.
66. "Looking Back at Tennessee."
67. "Vanishing Georgia," Georgia Department of Archives and History.
68. Cofield letter.
69. Connie Burkhalter, letter to author, June 22, 1990.
70. Joy Mahan, interview with author, January 3, 1990.
71. Mrs. Marcelle Coker White, letters to author, March 16, 1989 and July 2, 1991.
72. Ruby, 26–31.

Brain Dominance and Quilters: A Small Group Study

William J. Riffe

> ADVENTUROUS QUILTERS WANTED to form a study group. We would like to experiment with design, color, texture, and innovative construction techniques."

Would you respond to an open invitation to join a group doing things differently than others? Are you willing to try the unusual, the different, the creative? Eighteen people responded to the call and formed the group. In the three years since it began, several people left and others were asked to join the group. It is this final grouping that was the subject of a study of brain dominance with an eye toward understanding how these persons approached the quiltmaking task.

The basis of the brain dominance study was the Herrmann Brain Dominance Instrument.[1] It was administered to the group at one time. A final questionnaire (see Appendix A) was presented after the evaluation was complete but before the members knew the results of their evaluation.

The Evaluation Technique

The Herrmann Brain Dominance Instrument (HBDI) is a self-administered questionnaire of 120 questions. These questions con-

William J. Riffe is Professor and Director of Manufacturing Systems Engineering and teaches a course in creativity for engineers as well as technical engineering subjects. His creativity activities use the HBDI to help people understand themselves and the way they approach their profession and/or avocation. GMI Engineering & Management Institute, 1700 W. Third Avenue, Flint, MI 48504-4898.

cern the respondent's handedness, best and worst academic subjects, strength in sixteen different work element areas, self-descriptive adjectives, hobbies, energy level, susceptibility to motion sickness, descriptive adjective pairs, introversion versus extroversion, and then concludes with twenty questions asking for levels of agreement with the statements provided. Completion of the Instrument takes about thirty to forty-five minutes. After evaluation, the results were presented in both graphical and written form and were explained to each of the participants.

The Herrmann metaphor for brain dominance is based upon a four-quadrant scheme rather than the traditional left-brain versus right-brain model. The left brain is considered as containing the cerebral A-quadrant and the limbic B-quadrant. The right brain is considered as containing the limbic C-quadrant and the cerebral D-quadrant. The cerebral portion of the brain is considered the location of our reasoning and communication thinking. The limbic portion is the location of organizational and emotional thoughts.

In the HBDI, the upper left quadrant (called the A-quadrant) is considered as the location of typical logical, analytical, mathematical, technical, problem-solving thinking. The lower left quadrant (called the B-quadrant) is the location of controlled, conservative, planning, organizational, and administrative thinking style. The lower right quadrant (the C-quadrant) contains the thinking styles of interpersonal, emotional, musical, spiritual, and verbal. The upper right D-quadrant is the seat of imaginative, synthesizer, artistic, holistic, and conceptualizing thinking styles. For easy reference, these four quadrants may be considered as representing FACT (A), FORM (B), FEELINGS (C), and the FUTURE (D).

After scoring the Instrument, scores are divided into three groupings radiating from a central point. Scores between zero and thirty-three (0–33) indicate a low desire to act in that style but do not reflect an inability to perform in that style. These quadrants are given a notation of "3" to indicate this lower desire. For scores between thirty-four and sixty-six, (34–66), ease of use is assumed but this style of action is not prime. It is assigned a notation of "2". When the scores go above sixty-six (67–?), a notation of "1" is given to indicate the first choice of thinking style.

An individual's brain dominance and, therefore, the way in which he or she will act in a given situation is indicated by that person's Herrmann Brain Dominance Profile. For ease in discussing these profiles, they are described in terms of the 1-2-3 notation, so that a very analytical and conservative person might be described as a 1-1-2-3 while an emotional artistic person might carry a 3-2-1-1 designation. I will use this notation in this paper.

The Evaluation—Guessing Ahead

Before looking at the dominance results, it is instructive to generate a mental image of traditional quilts and the persons who make them. In this paper, traditional quilts will be considered as those that have blocks in various settings or are intended to portray a picture or an overall traditional design. These quilts may be considered as displaying precise forms, good organization, precision construction techniques, and sound logic. The geometric construction is such as to convey a recognizable form. All of these descriptors lead one to suspect that the traditional quiltmaker may be described by the brain dominance description of 1-1-2-2; strong in the left side activities of logic, fact, and form with lesser emphasis on feeling and innovation.

This is not to discount the role of creativity in the design and construction of the quilt, nor to reduce the influence of the feelings of the quiltmaker. It is just that the A-quadrant and B-quadrant styles overpower the effects of the C- and D-quadrants.

On the other hand, artist quiltmakers are looking less for a traditional pattern study and more toward using the product of their work as art. They attempt to marry the techniques used in quiltmaking with the artistic expression of a painter. The fabrics become the paint and the needle becomes the brush. Many of these works of art tend toward visual illusions, abstract shapes and color patterns, and symbolism of many forms. These quiltmakers stress the need for originality, creativity, and conveying a message or a feeling. Color plays a prominent role in the work that they do.

When geometric patterns are used, they are rarely used in a conventional sense. The logic may escape the viewer until the artist describes what is intended. Yet, similar to some traditional style quilts, underneath it all there is rhythm and form and harmony.

In terms of the HBDI, these latter quiltmakers could be described as 2-2-1-1. This is exactly the dominance style of the group that was studied. While each member of the group exhibits an individual style, the group as a whole exhibits a style as if they all function together.

The Evaluation—The HBDI

It is important to note that, while the individuals of the group range from the more traditional to the true artist, the predominant expression of quiltmaking is artistic. Thus, the group is not a microcosm of the historical world of quilters but may illustrate a major future world. As indicated in the group composite of Figure 1, every brain dominance is represented with many persons showing extreme mental dominance in the originality and creative D-quadrant.

In the A-quadrant, the average is 51 points and the range from maximum to minimum is 102 points with a heavy concentration of persons at the lower values. Without the two individuals at the extreme top, the group score would have been at the low end of the range in this quadrant. However, without these two persons, the group sometimes finds difficulty in those areas where technical problem solving and logic are required. These logic-basic individuals often become the teachers of techniques that are subsequently embellished by others.

The B-quadrant is only 67 points wide with an average of 60 points. This narrow range is to be expected as all quiltmakers must exhibit some sense of organization to make the pieces go together. Since some quilts, whether of traditional design or art pieces, contain over a thousand pieces, a lack of a sense of organization would spell disaster.

Feelings and color come from the C-quadrant where the spread is 75 points and the average is 79. Some individuals within this sample are finely attuned to color and the illusions that may be achieved with it, while others are more pictorial and true-to-life in

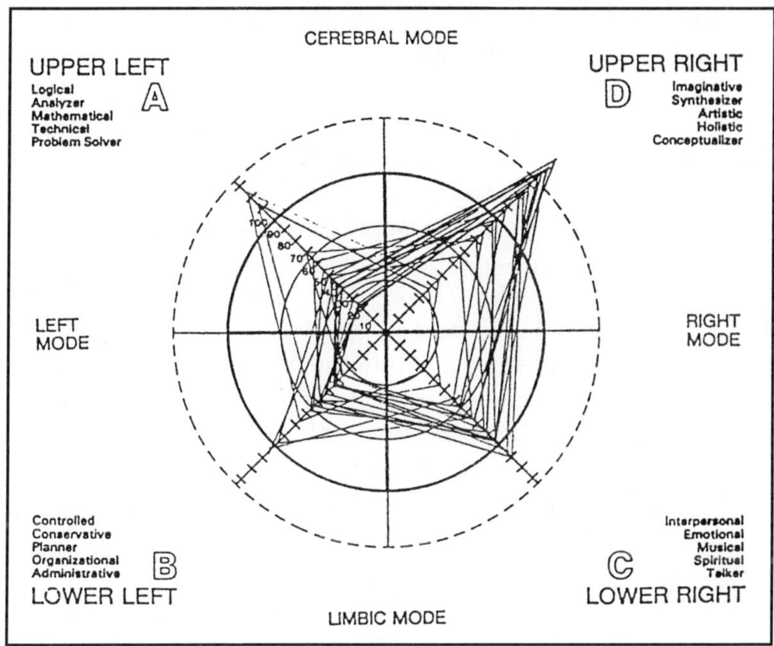

Figure 1. Group Composite for Adventurous Quilters, Herrmann Brain Dominance Profile. © Ned Herrmann, 1986.

their use of color. Brain dominance will not necessarily delineate this difference, but it will indicate the ability to recognize and express feelings and emotions. Color is just one means of their expression. A quilt conveys a sense of image and feeling of the quiltmaker. In traditional designs, expression is primarily by the choice of design and the fabrics used. For the art quilt, the overall image is the expression that is to be conveyed.

In the creative D-quadrant, an average of 105 belies the range of 105 points. Thus, it is safe to say that some respondents are creatively traditional while others are creative in a less traditional sense. It is also within this quadrant that one can see the diversity of styles in quiltmaking.

Excepting those two individuals who display strong A-quadrant styles, it should come as no surprise that quadrants A and B (Fact and Form) are narrow in spread from maximum to minimum. These two quadrants are the foundation of quiltmaking. It is only in recent years that quiltmaking as an art form (D-quadrant) has begun to achieve public acceptance.[2]

Noticing that the average score in each quadrant increases as one moves from A to B to C to D, further evidence is given that the group has strong tendencies toward very creative endeavors.

Part of the dominance evaluation asked the respondents to select eight adjectives from a list of twenty-five that "best describe the way you see yourself." The top three selected adjectives were artistic, intuitive, and imaginative. These are all not only right-mode characteristics but they are also associated with the D-quadrant of creativity. Following in order, but substantially lower in rating, are logical, emotional, detailed, reader, and simultaneous.

The choice of these particular adjectives is not surprising, considering the nature of the endeavor being evaluated. Quiltmaking, either in a traditional style or in the artistic style, is a whole-brain activity that involves all aspects of thinking style, but with some more dominant than others. And all of them occur simultaneously. The interest comes in the verification of these choices by the quiltmakers themselves.

Even greater contrast can be seen by looking at the lower end of the choice listing. These are factual, quantitative, and mathematical from the A-quadrant; conservative and controlled from the B-quadrant; and musical and spiritual from the C-quadrant. None of these is from the creative D-quadrant. The complete listing and their respective rankings are given in Figure 2.

Another section of the Instrument asked the respondent to "rate each of the work elements according to your strength in that activity." Sixteen choices are provided for which the respondent must rate a 5 for "work I do best" down to 1 for "work I do least well." Rating a score of 4.1 out of 5 for the group were creative and problem solving. Closely following these were implementation, planning, conceptualizing, integration, and organization. The bottom of the order were the elements administrative and financial. One could probably theorize that active, artistic quilters are not so much interested in business affairs, such as running a quilt shop, as they are in their artistic expression since the shop would detract from their time to quilt. The pure business aspects of administration and finance

Figure 2.
List of Key Descriptors

1. Artistic
2. Intuitive
3. Imaginative
4. Logical
5. Emotional
6. Detailed
7. Reader
8. Simultaneous
9. Holistic
10. Analytical
11. Rational
12. Synthesizer
13. Spatial
14. Verbal
15. Symbolic
16. Dominant
17. Critical
18. Sequential
19. Spiritual
20. Controlled
21. Mathematical
22. Quantitative
23. Factual
24. Conservative
25. Musical

Figure 3.
List of Work Elements

Creative
Problem solving
Implementation
Conceptualizing
Integration
Teaching
Planning
Innovating
Organized
Analytical
Expressing
Technical
Writing
Interpersonal
Administrative
Financial

are either not to their liking or intentionally subordinated to the pleasure received from quiltmaking. A complete listing of the work elements and their ranking is given in Figure 3.

One could now piece together a very reasonable picture of the "average" member of this particular quilting group; however, remember that this small group is not necessarily indicative of all or even many such groups. Also, traits associated with particular brain dominances are only traits and are not absolute. Each person exhibits traits from all quadrants and it is only the particular combination of those traits that leads to dominance. The average member is a woman who enjoys blending the techniques of quiltmaking and of the art world to create artistic expressions. These may be functional as bed quilts or clothing, or may be more artistic such as wall quilts, commercial or liturgical art. In either use, the piece will display the unique capabilities of the maker as creative artist and less of the traditional quilt genre. These persons have deep emotions which are expressed in color and images.

A look at the workspace and storage area of some of these people would be expected to display the same breadth of organization as the dominance. Those with a dominance that is anything but the far right generally would exhibit the trait of organization of their fabrics. These may not be precisely organized but would be grouped in such a manner as to greatly facilitate retrieval of the desired fabric. For the extreme far right dominant people, the fabric may be in apparent disarray with many projects in motion simultaneously. There may be two or three major projects in various states of completion with others as just piles of papers and material. Ask for a particular piece of information or fabric and the only one who could possibly find it would be the person who "filed" it. What appears to be disorganization is, in reality, just an unconventional form of organization.

The "quilt stash" of the typical quiltmaker is probably grouped by color, if it is grouped at all. It will contain a variety of prints and color meanderings, most selected because they were interesting and called out to become part of the collection. Some will be hand-dyed. Others will probably represent the broadest spectrum of fabrics available. Also included might be some lamé, some Japanese kasuri or shibori, some batik, some baubles and beads, ribbon, and other trimmings.

The above description of the average quiltmaker is based upon the traits associated with the average dominance displayed by the group and should not be viewed as being characteristic of all quiltmakers of that dominance. Just as persons are not capable of being placed into narrowly defined groupings, neither should the subset "quiltmakers" be subject to such categorization. The dominances provide for understanding persons by looking through a telescope, not a microscope. There is much diversity within any particular style.

Supplemental Questionnaire

A supplemental questionnaire inquired specifically about quilting activities, and did not delve further into the dominance. It was then correlated with the dominance responses. The results were very supportive of the dominance influence. The entire questionnaire is attached as an Appendix.

When asked for their preferred design method, respondents with strong left-mode tendencies indicated that they use traditional blocks in traditional or non-traditional ways. As the dominance moved further to the right, the trend was away from traditional blocks toward non-traditional blocks or a non-block style. These designs start out as a sketch but eventually become a scaled drawing, if for no other reason than to make templates.

Inspiration for works comes from many sources with photos and magazine articles as a primary inspiration for quiltmakers from all quadrants. The more adventurous may also have a mental image that needs to come to life or they may allow the fabric to lead to the design. The continuum from analytical and logical organization (A,B-quadrants) toward the ethereal (C,D-quadrants) is visibly demonstrated by this group.

Visual effects are sometimes planned in detail but often just evolve as the pieces are joined. The trick is to "see" what is happening and take steps to heighten the illusion. This is certainly a right-mode creative activity.

Fabric is bought in no unique way. Some buy color, some buy design, some buy because it is interesting. When used, this fabric is often joined by other materials bought to complete the project or by hand-dyed fabrics.

Plastic templates are a favorite of all but the most right-mode people who prefer the versatility and ease of freezer-paper templates. The rationality of this becomes apparent when one considers that the traditional blocks lend themselves to repetitive patterns which are facilitated by plastic templates. The non-block works often contain pieces which are all unique and non-repetitive, making the hard plastic templates practically useless. The rotary cutter has made the freezer paper approach a simple, effective, and fast process.

After cutting, most projects are machine pieced because of the time savings attendant to that process. From there, either hand or machine quilting is done, again depending upon the time factor and the suitability of the design, or upon the ease of the quilter with machine quilting. Those who have become proficient in machine quilting are enthusiastic about its suitability for most work.

An attempt was made to look at the interpersonal relationships of these quilters by asking whether the acceptance of their work by others was important. While there is universal concern for acceptance, it does not seem to be an overwhelming concern. This is probably what allows some of these quilters to experiment with new techniques.

The B-quadrant organizational aspects come through again when discussing the work area and fabric storage area. The more left-mode describe their areas as very organized while the right-mode describe theirs as "Federal Disaster Areas."

When asked to indicate the number of quilt classes taken or taught in the last two years, there is no discernible trend. This can be the result of family concerns (child care) or economic conditions (employment). It could also be an indication that classes for the advanced, original quiltmaker are just not available locally. In terms of classes taught, the group is at either end of the scale—either nonteachers or teaching a large percentage of the time, and when teaching, the classes are primarily the traditional-type quiltmaking classes.

When asked to indicate who in the group is most like them in quiltmaking style where comparison is made with the finished article and not by whether the article is pieced or appliqued, the relationships are so diverse that no trend or inference can be made. (This diversity of relationships is probably the key to the success of the group. There is no one style or technique that predominates and thus all can learn and benefit from the group activities.)

Everyone would like to be remembered for something that they have done and quiltmakers are no exception. When asked to describe their "ultimate creation," they again mirrored the wide range of styles described above by stating:

- "my heirloom sampler, a very precisely, well executed piece";
- "a very geometric quilt with optical illusion using stripes and colors to create a moving kaleidoscope";
- "a scrap quilt, the challenge is to make color work to create feelings from color";
- "a semi-abstract pictorial collage with lots of visual effects—metallic bead-

ing, embroidery, textures, that can be looked at again and again and not see everything going on";
- "an original, with a new technique using custom-made fabric".

These are actual quotes from the quiltmakers in left-to-right order. One can easily see the transition from logical organization to the creative and unconventional.

Anecdotal Evidence

As in any group of persons seeking to learn with and from others, the group dynamics are important. First and foremost in a group such as this is the factor of trust. While these quiltmakers may compete with one another in local or national shows, that competitiveness is not apparent in the small group. When asked, the group provides critique in a constructive and helpful manner. As an outsider viewing this group, it is readily apparent that a very high level of trust is evident.

An example of this is evidenced by a typical "I would like some advice on this situation . . ." question brought to the group by one member. She had constructed a set of sampler blocks, thirty-one in all, for which she desired a top using any thirty (6 blocks x 5 blocks). They were placed upon the floor in a somewhat random order and the group proceeded to arrange and rearrange the blocks until an acceptable pattern was achieved. The requester was near the midpoint in the listing of the group members from most left to most right. The assistance she received came primarily from the persons who were most left and most right. The most right were concerned with color balance while the most left were concerned with block pattern organization. The requester had placed her trust in the group and they had responded. Her sampler top now had the benefit of the broad range of capabilities that diverse brain dominances can provide, yet it remains hers in concept, fabric selection, and construction.

In terms of collaboration, an interesting arrangement is in effect with the two individuals who exhibit the most right and most left thinking styles according to the HBDI. These two women are long-time friends and have built a very high level of mutual trust. Each is an accomplished quiltmaker who has done many commissioned pieces. While they critique each other's work, they also work in collaboration. The most right does the design and color selection while the most left develops the most efficient way to construct the piece. It is then a rush to the finish such that, as the designer operates the sewing machine, the organizer hands her pieces to sew. The process goes very well since both are performing the tasks that they enjoy doing best and for which they have the brain dominance. In terms of brain dominance, it seems that the A- and D-quadrants are not at opposite ends of the spectrum but only in adjacent positions on a circular continuum.

Conclusions

This study of a small group of quiltmakers should not be considered as a study of the world of quiltmakers. The participants were self-selected on the basis of their interest in looking at innovative quiltmaking techniques and not the traditional techniques. While the group contained members with a broad scope of dominances, the majority of the group were distinctly right-mode dominant.

Those who produce the artistic-style quilts display the self-descriptors of artistic, intuitive, and imaginative thinking from the right side dominance, but also display the strong characteristics of logical and detailed thinking from the left. They consider themselves creative but also quite expert at problem solving, a combination of left and right mode functions.

In general, it may be said that the quiltmaker whose works are artistic in style rather than traditional will display a right mode thinking dominance (2-2-1-1) according to the Herrmann Brain Dominance model while those who produce the more traditional works will display a left mode thinking dominance (1-1-2-2).

Beyond the details of this study, the individuals of the group also gained some insight into their own approach to quiltmaking, and into how they related to others who perform a similar activity. Two areas of understanding are worthy of note here. First, each came to understand that the way in which they conceive, design, and construct a quilt is valid for them, and that others of similar dominance would probably use a similar technique. Satisfaction and comfort in their own style is important. Secondly, the way other quiltmakers create a masterpiece is unique to them and need not be copied if the process of making such an article is not comfortable. The field of quiltmaking is large enough to encompass all styles of work as they reflect the diverse brain dominance patterns of the creators.

In terms of the group, they recognized the value of surrounding themselves with people of diverse styles so that advantage can be taken of the natural breadth of brain dominances. "Strength through diversity" applies to quiltmaking as well as most other activities that people undertake. The group certainly supports the name that they have adopted: "ADVENTUROUS QUILTERS."

Notes

1. Ned Herrmann, *The Creative Brain*, (Lake Lure, NC: Brain Books, 1988).
2. Penny McMorris and Michael Kile, *The Art Quilt*, (San Francisco, CA: Quilt Digest Press, 1986).

Appendix A. Adventurous Quilters Group Analysis Style

Please answer the questions below by placing the numbers 1, 2, 3 or 4 as appropriate in front of the responses that apply. Space has been provided to write in answers where this is necessary. In question 14, please write as descriptively as possible.

1. When you design quilts, do you
   (__) use traditional blocks in traditional ways
   (__) use traditional blocks in non-traditional ways
   (__) use non-traditional blocks
   (__)

2. The inspiration for your quilts comes from
   (__) magazine articles
   (__) photo
   (__) design studies
   (__) contest rules
   (__)

3. When you have a mental image of what you want in a quilt design, do you
   (__) make a sketch
   (__) draw it to scale
   (__)

4. When special visual effects are desired, you
   (__) plan in detail
   (__) plan only one area at a time
   (__)

5. In deciding what colors to use for your work, do you
   (__) use what is on hand
   (__) buy what is needed from the store
   (__) create the material using special techniques
   (__)

6. When buying material, do you
   (__) buy for a special project
   (__) buy to complete a color grouping
   (__) buy because it is interesting
   (__)

7. When preparing to cut out the pieces of material, do you
   (__) use a plastic template
   (__) use a paper template
   (__) use freezer paper patterns
   (__)

8. During assembly of a quilt, do you
   (__) hand piece and hand quilt
   (__) hand piece and machine quilt
   (__) machine piece and hand quilt
   (__) machine piece and machine quilt

9. How concerned are you about the acceptance of your work by your peers?
   (__) greatly concerned
   (__) somewhat concerned
   (__) very little concerned

10. The area where your work and keep your textiles would be described as
   (__) very organized, items are easy to find
   (__) grouped but no formal organization
   (__) Federal Disaster Area

11. During the past two years, the number of quilt classes taken is (pick one category only)
   (__) 0 to 2
   (__) 3 to 6
   (__) 7 to 12
   (__) more than 12

12. During the past two years, the number of different quilt classes taught has been (pick one category only)
   (__) 0 to 2 different classes
   (__) 3 to 6 different classes
   (__) more than 6 different classes

13. Within this quilt group, the one person that is most like you in quilting style is

14. In the space below, describe for me your "ultimate creation", the one you would like to be remembered for.

Mary A. McElwain: Quilter and Quilt Businesswoman

Pat L. Nickols

Mary A. McElwain (1869–1943) was a talented needlewoman; although skilled in many types of handwork, her first love was quilts. She learned to make quilts as a young girl, taught others to quilt, collected quilts, designed quilts, and established a shop for those who wanted to buy quilts or make their own.

The business that grew to become the Mary A. McElwain Quilt Shop was located in Walworth, Wisconsin, a small town in the southern part of an agricultural area, sixty miles from Milwaukee, seventy miles from Madison, the state capital, and eighty miles from Chicago, Illinois.[1] (Figure 1) The jewelry and watch repair shop, run by Mary and William McElwain, was located on a corner of the village square, a central open green area, one of many stores that framed the square. This central location was where the active businesses of the village of Walworth were located. The local paper, *The Walworth Times*, reported, "In 1912 they started a business here, which was given over to jewelry and watch repairing as Mr. McElwain's part and a gift shop over which Mrs. McElwain presided."[2] The gift area of the shop sold colorful glassware and dishes, and in one corner a small needlework display included knitted, crocheted, embroidered, and quilted articles. These finished items, made by Mary and local Walworth area women, were for sale as were patterns and the necessary supplies for customers who wished to make their own needlework. If customers needed instruction in the various needle skills,

---

Pat L. Nickols is a quiltmaker, quilting instructor, and a committed quilt researcher. This is her third contribution to *Uncoverings*. Box 9607, Rancho Santa Fe, CA 92067.

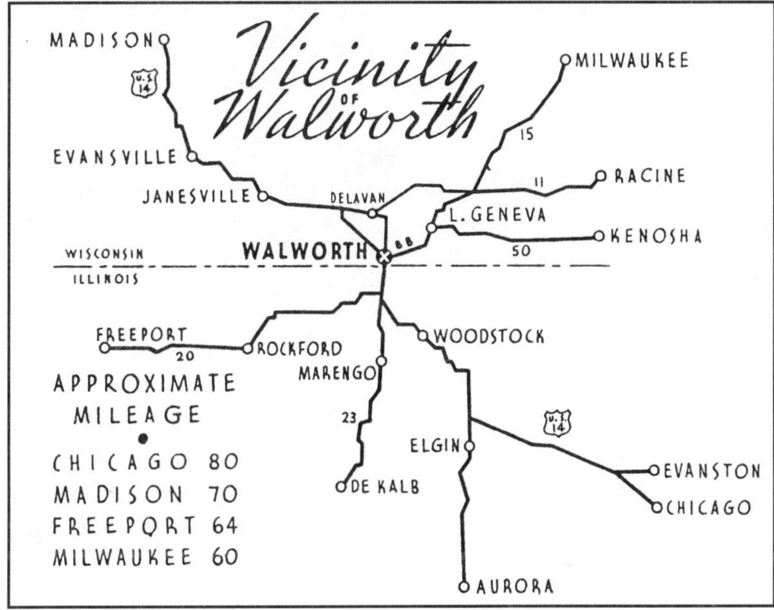

Figure 1. All Roads Lead to Walworth. This map, featured on page two of the McElwain catalog, gave visitors clear directions to the McElwain Quilt Shop.

Mary gave lessons in her helpful way, always aiming for the best possible stitchery to give the maker pride and satisfaction in her finished piece. She sought out products to insure her customers of quality needle craft, whether they were purchasing Marie Webster quilt patterns, Peter Pan fabrics, Stiles Waxt thread, Rock River Two Star batting, Boag or Comfy quilt kits, or her completed quilts.[3]

This successful business venture which Mary created with much support and help from family and friends can be more easily understood if we look at Mary herself. (Figure 2.) Her pioneer parents, Hiram Alyger (1836–1887) born in Amsterdam, New York, and Annie Jane Boyd (1847–1935) born in Ireland, were married in 1865 in Elmira, New York, following his discharge from service in the Civil War. They moved west, first to Marion, Iowa, where Mary was born in 1869, and then to Sanborn, Iowa. Here her father started his business of building homes, erecting the first house in Sanborn, and, with his crew of carpenters, he began building settlements in O'Brien County, Iowa. Her Irish mother was a hard worker who loved to help everyone in the community Her Irish grandmother, Mary A. Pogue Alyger, was both a doctor, first in Irelend, then in Amsterdam, New York, and last in Sanborn, Iowa, and also a quiltmaker who taught her daughter Annie and namesake granddaughter, Mary, the art of quiltmaking.[4] Mary Ann Alyger grew up in Sanborn and taught school before her marriage in 1890 to William E. McElwain. Their daughter DeEtte was born in 1892 and son Lloyd in 1897.[5] William McElwain worked for the railroad in Sanborn and continued railroad work when they moved to Walworth, Wisconsin, in 1900, becoming a member of the "Milk Train Crew." Milk and dairy products, the major cash crops from this area were sent by train to Chicago on the rail line that ran through Walworth, and experienced train men were given the prestigious "milk train runs." Leaving his railroad duties in 1912, William McElwain opened a small jewelry and watch repair shop with his wife Mary.[6] She was very involved in school activities with their children, as well as in the Congregational Church where she was Sunday School superintendent for twenty years. She was also an officer of the Order of Eastern Star. Their son Lloyd (1897–1979) married in 1918, and daughter-in-law Nettie Edington (1895–1991) was a welcome addition to the McElwain family, as were granddaughters Virginia, born in 1919, and Mary Ellen, born in 1924. Virginia recalls that "during the week Grandma had a housekeeper but Sunday evening was special. She liked to cook when our family came for dinner." Family was very important to Mary, and while all of the family helped with her quilting business, she in turn always made them feel very special by finding time to be with them.[7] The successful shop attracted Walworth friends and neighbors, shoppers from nearby towns and the large cities of Milwaukee and Chicago, and even customers from abroad. Mary needed help supplying the needlework items and developed a Womens' Exchange, at one time employing sixty local women who made a wide variety of afghans, aprons, pillows, and other items, as well as quilts. They would cut, baste, or sew sample blocks of applique or pieced work, quilt, and bind quilts.[8] Both granddaughters enjoyed working in the shop after school and during summer vaca-

Figure 2. Mary Ann Alyger McElwain (1869–1943) Needlewoman, quilt-maker, quilt collector and quilt designer. Shown here in her garden, Mary loved flowers, people and quilts. Photo courtesy of Virginia Hueschen, granddaughter of Mary McElwain.

tions, straightening shelves, cleaning glass shelves, and sorting money into the cash register, but they also enjoyed taking the train with their grandmother on buying trips to the Chicago Merchandise Mart where Mary selected gift items for the shop. Granddaughter Mary Ellen tells of delivering packages to workers in town, for which she was paid five cents a package, even if three packages went to the same house. Completed work was brought back to her grandmother to be incorporated into kits, packaged for sale, or to satisfy orders for finished quilts.[9] Some work was also sent to quilters in Kentucky, an active area for needlework cottage industries.[10]

In the 1920s William McElwain or "Mr. Mac," as he was called by those who worked with him, approached retirement. His jewelry and watch repair business had declined, more stores had opened, and increased train and car transportation was available so that his customers had more opportunity to shop in the surrounding large cities. However, the quilt-related part of the business had expanded, and Mary saw the need for more space to accommodate the growing number of customers who came to see walls lined with quilts and shelves filled with pillow covers, quilt kits, quilt patterns, quilting templates, and afghans. Once comprising only a few items in a corner of the jewelry store, the volume of quilts, patterns, and other needlework had grown. "The quilts pushed everything else out," stated DeEtte McElwain Robars, as she told of the history of the shop in a 1937 newspaper interview.[11]

William retired in the early 1930s, closing the watch repair and jewelry business part of the shop, but the gift shop continued as the Mary A. McElwain Quilt Shop. William McElwain ran the busy shipping department and often helped with the bookkeeping.

An article in *The Walworth Times* in the fall of 1933 reported

> Over five hundred guests attended the opening . . . two new quilt designs were shown, an applique quilt called, "The Gay Garden" and one in patchwork called "The American Tapestry." Tea was served both days and Miss Jean Radebough sang old fashioned songs to her own melodeon accompaniment.

The article noted that the needed expansion was completed:

> The studio enlarges the Quilt shop to more than double the space used before . . . a double archway has been cut through from the original

shop to the studio. Mrs. McElwain states it had become a necessity . . . because of the many visitors who came in such large groups it was almost impossible to accommodate them in the small space available. It will be possible now to exhibit quilts to clubs in the studio here rather than take the display to another city to the club. This cuts down expense and labor for the Quilt shop and expense for the club."[12]

This expansion was done in the Great Depression, a difficult time for farm-based communities, nearby small manufacturing towns, and the large cities of Milwaukee and Chicago, the areas where most of McElwain's customers lived. However, many of her customers were wealthy patrons who seemed unaffected by the Depression, and their purchases of expensive giftwares as well as finished quilts gave Mary the financial ability to grow. Mary, her daughter DeEtte, and others had taken quilts and staged exhibits for women's groups and clubs in the nearby towns of Beloit, Racine, Janesville, and Madison, Wisconsin, and Rockford and Chicago, Illinois. They had traveled great distances to hold exhibits in St. Petersburg, Florida, and Washington, D. C.[13] The quilt shop grew and prospered during difficult times—both the first World War and the lean times surrounding the Great Depression.[14] The McElwains expanded the shop in 1933, but even with the success of the shop Mary was aware of the need for cost-cutting measures. Sales could be maintained, or even increased, if instead of taking her quilts out to exhibit, visitors could come to see shop displays and become customers for quilts, quilt findings, and fine gifts.

The January 1933 issue of *Hobbies* magazine gave readers a summary of one of Mrs. McElwain's recent broadcasts over radio station WLS: "The basis for the facts presented in this quilt talk came from '*Quilts; Their Story and How to Make Them*,' by Marie Webster; '*Old Patchwork Quilts and the Women Who Made Them*,' by Ruth E. Finley; '*Old Fashioned Quilts*,' by Carlie Sexton, and '*Patchwork Quilts*' by Clementine Paddleford, from *Farm and Fireside* and the *Country Home*. Each book should have a place in every library." Even during these lean times McElwain felt it was necessary that these quilt books be in her listeners' homes. She gave a picturesque history of the early pioneer days, quilts, and the women who made them. "So you see, quilting was a necessary labor, but the quilter made it an art. She traced and stitched as she worked in to these quilts her hopes and dreams from the scraps of cloth just as housewives of today exchange recipes and crochet patterns. Together they admire scraps of calico, as cloth was scarce and tiny pieces were saved, exchanged and worked into patchwork." With the Depression all around them farm and urban listeners alike welcomed this romantic tale. "Mrs. McElwain says her clientele, coming sometimes two hundred miles to visit her quilt shop, tell her it is like wandering through an old art gallery or an old fashioned garden, whose fragrance is reminiscent of stories of yesteryear."[15]

Ruth W. Peterson, of Rockford, Illinois, tells of frequent visits she and her mother made to the Quilt Shop and how they enjoyed seeing the displays of quilts layered on the beds. In the late 1930s Ruth picked out a tiny blue print for the Pride of the Forest quilt her mother offered to make. After her mother passed away Ruth brought the completed blocks back to the shop to have a quilt made. When it was finished Mrs. McElwain suggested she have a dated inscription with her name and that of her mother put on the back of the quilt in small black cross stitch. The cost of the inscription was around two dollars.[16]

Jenny Furvor Neville (1869–1951), of Grays Lake, Illinois, looked forward to Saturday afternoons when her daughter Alta finished work and would drive her up to Walworth see the quilts at the McElwain Quilt Shop. Jenny had learned to make traditional geometric quilts from her mother, Merub Barron Furvor. After the six Neville children were grown Jenny returned to quiltmaking about 1930, and she loved the numerous floral applique patterns she found at the McElwain Quilt Shop. Neville made over forty-five quilts, including the Daisy Chain, an applique pattern Mary designed.[17] Daisy Chain, a favorite of McElwain's, was featured on the cover of Mary's book, *Romance of the Village Quilts*, and was available stamped for \$12.50, cut for \$12.50, basted for \$25.00, or finished for \$85.00. Most paper patterns were 35 cents, ready-cut quilts (kits) were about \$12.00 and finished quilts ranged from \$50.00 for the Rainbow Star, Log Cabin, and Grandmother's Fancy to \$85.00 for the Horn Of Plenty, Romance, and Indiana Wreath.

International visitors and prominent Americans visited the shop.

Mrs. Olaf Bernts, wife of the consul of Norway has the Golden Poppy quilt," noted a newspaper article of May 1930, and "Mrs. Chauncy Blair of Paris purchased the Wreath of Leaves quilt, two other quilts and several pillows to take back to Paris with her and exhibit some of them as examples of American artwork. Here in the United States Mr. and Mrs. John D. Rockefeller, Jr. came to Walworth and purchased two quilts and Mrs. Frank O. Lowden wife of the ex-governor of Illinois is a customer. . . . 'Heirlooms of tomorrow,' is what Mrs. Mary McElwain calls her eighteen year old hobby of quiltmaking which has grown from a meager project to a flourishing business.[18]

Mary McElwain's love of people, needle skills, hard work, and romantic outlook drew visitors who then became customers. Although quilts were the attraction, the purchase of expensive giftware contributed to the financial success of the shop. The Walworth Bank sent teller, Charlotte Belland, over to the quilt shop to help prepare the bank deposit when Mary was ill. Belland recalled: "it was interesting to see checks come to the McElwain shop from all over the country and even other countries."[19]

In March 1933, the Garden Club of Illinois invited McElwain to exhibit quilts at the Chicago Navy Pier as part of their display of gardens and flowers. She had often given programs for their meetings, and the clubs had sent bus loads of members to see her shop.[20]

It was no surprise that McElwain, a well-known quilt authority, was selected as one of five judges for the National Sears Century of Progress Quilt contest to be held in Chicago in June 1933. (Figure 3) The other judges, all recognized experts, were Robert B. Harshe, Director of The Chicago Art Institute; Anne Orr, Needlework Editor, *Good Housekeeping* magazine; Sue Roberts, Home Advisor, Sears Roebuck and Company; and Mrs. Charles W. Sewell, Director of Home and Community Work for the American Farm Bureau Federation.[21]

The Grand National Prize of $1,000 was won by Miss Margaret Rogers Caden, Lexington, Kentucky, for the Feathered Star quilt she entered but apparently did not make. Mattie Black did the piecing and several of the women that worked for Miss Caden did the quilting. This Grand Prize winning quilt was then presented to first lady Eleanor Roosevelt.[22] Margaret Schuldt, who worked in the McElwain store for many years, remembers Mrs. Roosevelt's visits

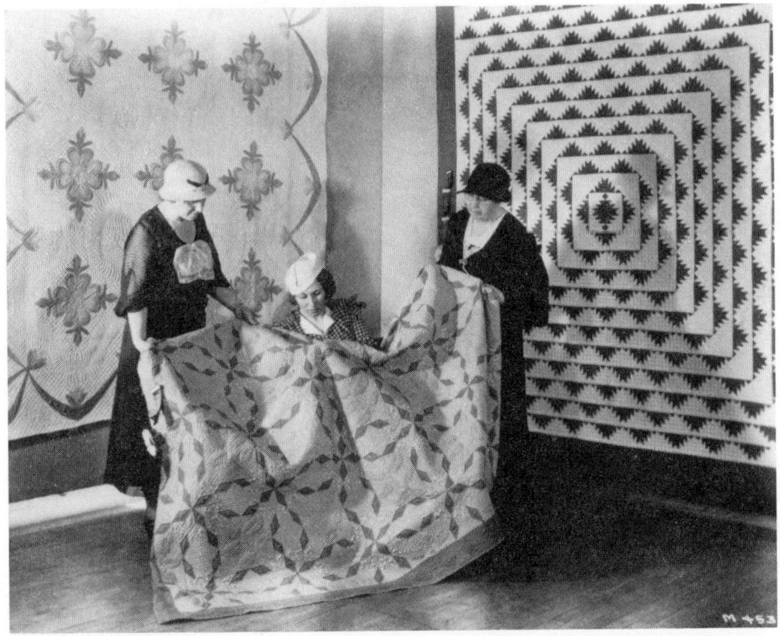

Figure 3. The winning quilts in Sears Century of Progress Quilt Contest, at the 1933 World's Fair held in Chicago. Judges examine the Feathered Star quilt, Grand National Prize Winner from more than 15,000 entries. Mary McElwain is shown on the right. Photo courtesy of Sears, Roebuck and Company.

to the store while visiting her son at a nearby military academy and "how we were always on our best behavior then," for this special customer.[23]

Mary wrote *The Romance of the Village Quilts* which was published in 1936 by The Daily News Publishing Company, Beloit, Wisconsin. (Figure 4) Mary knew needlework and had high standards of workmanship for herself and those who worked for her. She so appreciated her quilting help that she dedicated her first literary effort to the "courage, skill and patience . . . of the dear hands that made the quilts. . . . God bless their dear hands." The thirty-five page book, filled with McElwain's philosophy, history she had gathered, quilt illustrations, products, and price list became a desirable catalog for

Figure 4. Cover of *Romance of the Village Quilts* the nostalgic 1936 catalog written by Mary A. McElwain which illustrated some of the numerous quilts and products available at her shop.

quiltmakers and those who admired McElwain's quilts. Her book was also enjoyed by homemakers who loved quilts but did not make them. This publication was available at the shop for twenty-five cents or by mail from Rock River Batting Company, Janesville, Illinois.[24]

The shop carried a wide variety of quilt styles and patterns. Quilts were displayed in the main room of the shop layered on two antique beds—one featuring pieced quilts and the other applique styles. After viewing the quilt displays or reading the catalog customers could purchase paper patterns for thirty-five cents, a kit with the pieces already cut for about twelve dollars, a basted applique quilt for about twenty dollars, or a finished quilt for about sixty dollars. All of the necessary quilt supplies, such as fabric, thread, needles, batting, quilting stencils, and transparent rulers were available from the McElwain shop or by mail order. Metal cutting patterns backed with sandpaper were available in four sizes for squares or hexagons. About thirty quilt patterns were offered through the catalog but many more were shown hanging on the walls of the shop. McElwain favored Marie Webster patterns and stocked them from the 1920s until the end of the 1950s.

Illustrations in the book indicate that some patterns were McElwain's own designs, while others were derived from other sources. Daisy Chain, the quilt pictured on the cover of her book, was her own creation and was known to be one of her favorites. Double Irish Chain was described, "as arranged by Mary A. McElwain Quilt Shop, Walworth, Wisc." (Figure 5) Horn Of Plenty was used by permission of the *Home Arts Needlecraft Magazaine*. The Laurel, Rose of 1840, Baby Star, Quilt of a Thousand Prints, and Muscatel Grape were identified as patterns copied from antique quilts, "made over one hundred years ago." Grandmother's Fancy, a floral and bird applique medallion-style pattern copied from an early nineteenth-century southeastern Iowa quilt, was available basted for $20.00 or finished for $50.00 in 1936, but the source was not noted. The quilt tops and finished quilts of this pattern were actually made by Lillian Walker (1870–1969) of Fairfied, Iowa, who worked for Mary and went on become a well-known, one-woman quilt industry of her own. Widowed in 1924, with a young son to raise, Walker turned to quiltmaking, and her successful venture found her employing women

Figure 5. Double Irish Chain, illustrated on page five of the McElwain catalog, as "arranged by Mary A. McElwain," was also in the set of eleven tissue paper patterns sold by Rock River Batting Company.

in Iowa, Kentucky, Missouri, and Minnesota to help her fill the many orders for quilts.[25]

Indiana Wreath, a floral applique medallion-style quilt, was copied from the frontispiece of *Quilts: Their Story and How To Make Them* by Marie D. Webster. This book, published in 1915, was the first book on American quilt history. The author, in addition to writing a well-researched historical overview, was also a successful designer of beautiful applique quilt patterns. Mary McElwain sold Webster patterns, and Mary's book shows many examples of Webster quilts hanging on the walls of the shop in the photographs featuring different quilt patterns.[26]

Some patterns illustrated in McElwain's attractive catalog were variations of patterns by other designers. For example the A B C Crib Quilt illustrated on page twenty-three of her catalog has the same arrangement and some of the same motifs as "Alphabet," a 1930 Nancy Page pattern. Changing parts of patterns or doing a different arrangement was as common then as it is now. A very similar A B C crib quilt won first place as an "original design" in the National Quilting Association's Fourth Annual Quilt Show in 1973.[27] Grace Cox Swanson, while living in Battle Creek, Michigan, made a A B C crib quilt in 1931 for her son, Bob. Her basic pattern could have been from McElwain. The alternating blue and white sashing and multiple borders were designed by her mother Martha.[28] When visitors brought antique quilts to the McElwain shop Mary would often sketch different design elements to add to her collection. She traced some blocks of antique quilts, and these paper patterns were made up in fabric as sample blocks for Mary by the women who worked in the shop.

Mary McElwain made effective use of publicity and advertising in marketing her quilts and other gift items. She put on quilt exhibits, and presented radio quilt talks, both on WCLO, the local Janesville radio station, and on WLS in Chicago. She wrote an article for *Hobbies* magazine titled, "Quilts, Heirlooms of Tomorrow," and she judged quilt shows. Certainly judging the Sears Century of Progress Quilt Show gave her publicity beyond any advertising she could have done.[29] There is no evidence that she took out display ads in newspapers; instead, she used personal appearances as well as newspaper articles about her quilt exhibits to generate interest in her shop. Mary stated her philosophy in this way: "A successful business venture is merely the outcome of a hobby, a natural ability used in serious life."[30] Robert Markiewitz, a salesman for Collingbourne Mills, Elgin, Illinois, who sold thread and die-cut quilt kits to the McElwain shop, said, "Everyone liked her, I never heard a bad word about her." His wife, Josephine Douthitt Markiewitz, (1907–1982) was a quiltmaker who liked piecing and applique, making over forty-five tops. A number of her tops were quilted and bound by the McElwain shop, as "she didn't like that part," according to her husband.

Mary's employees and suppliers were also her customers. The local women she employed in her cottage industry also purchased kits, fabric, and other quilt findings for their own use. When they needed gifts of stemware and fine dishes for wedding gifts, anniversaries, or other special occasions, they bought these items from her shop rather than go to stores in larger cities. Mary selected quality products for her shop noting "the superiority of the brands" she carried. Her catalog offered some of these products, often devoting a full page of advertising for companies such as Rock River Cotton Company, Janesville, Wisconsin. Their products featured Two Star Fine China batting, "very easily quilted," mattress pads, and down pillows. The same company purchased quilt patterns from her which they sold in a foldover set of eleven tissue-paper patterns. In 1919, the price for the set was ten cents, available by mail order from Rock River. They also enclosed a length of several patterns with each roll of batting.[33] All of these patterns stated "Pattern furnished through the courtesy of Mary A. McElwain Quilt Shop, Walworth, Wisconsin." These patterns could be purchased from her shop or by sending twenty-five cents to Rock River. She then had her advertising reaching quiltmakers with every purchase of Rock River batting or quilt patterns.

In April 1952, Rock River Cotton Company sold their equipment, inventories and material to Lockport Cotton Batting Company, Lockport, New York. The same McElwain patterns were then sold by Lockport. In September 1960, Mrs. W. B. Ellis wrote to Rock River Cotton Company asking for quilt patterns she had seen advertised in the *Ladies Home Journal.* The company still had some patterns and replied that they were sending her the folder of eleven patterns but they were interested in the advertisement. "No one here can remember when we did magazine advertising. Could you tell us the date?" She thanked them for their reply, noting the patterns had not as yet arrived, and sent back the date from the magazine—November 1919. Mary had indeed selected a quality service-oriented batting company which could fill a pattern request forty-one years after the ad appeared in a magazine and eight years after they sold the company![34]

The McElwain catalog states "the shop uses Stiles Waxt Thread exclusively. It is a six cord waxed spool cotton especially adapted for fine hand sewing that DOES NOT KNOT." The smooth wax treatment made it easier to sew and to thread a needle. "The process by which this thread is treated is the unique invention of a woman, who realized the trials of sewing with ordinary spool cotton." The Stiles Waxt Thread Company of Sycamore, Illinois, purchased thread spun by Coats Thread company which was wound on small one-half inch wooden spools.[35] These spools were then wax-treated by Mrs. Stiles and her family.[36] Mary selected "Genuine, Guaranteed Fast Color, PETER PAN, Ginghams, Percales, Plain Colors, and Prints," for her finished quilts and for her customers, as she had found fabric manufactured by this company to be the very best for quiltmaking. The soft texture was easy to work with, it took the needle readily, the yarn produced threads that resisted wear, and it was moderately priced. Peter Pan could supply the newest colors each season as well as the dependable staple colors.

"Cut,""ready cut," and "die cut" pieces were the terms used to describe accurately cut fabric pieces in what we now call quilt kits. Over a dozen of McElwain's patterns listed in the catalog were available, each as a "ready cut quilt top" for quiltmakers who didn't want to make templates, purchase fabric, and mark and cut fabric before they could start stitching their quilts. The box for an applique quilt contained all background material, applique pieces, folded bias stemming, binding, and one basted block for the quiltmaker to follow. These quilt kits were priced about twelve dollars in 1936. The die-cutting company which supplied the fabric quilt pieces, was owned by George Boag, of River Forest, Illinois. He trimmed the corners of the triangle templates so that quilters could avoid excess fabric at the points when joining multiple pieces. Boag sold the company to Collingbourne Mills in the 1930s; and when Collingbourne went out of business in the late 1930s they sold to Robert Markiewitz. Markiewitz ran the company, renamed Comfy Products, Chicago, Illinois, from his basement until the early 1940s when it was closed, due to war-time difficulties in obtaining fabric. Many years later, in 1985, he sold the company to Hearthside Quilts, Shelburne, Vermont, where many of the same die-cut patterns seen in the McElwain catalog and Boag catalog can be purchased today.[37]

If you were to take a trip back in time to the 1930s you would drive up to Walworth, as countless people did, when you wanted to buy a quilt or to make one yourself. The small bell above the door tinkled as you entered, and you were immediately greeted by Mary, a member of her family, or other employees, with a gracious welcome, as though you had come for a social visit. The first thing you saw was her large doll collection displayed in floor-to-ceiling glass cases. Shelves were filled with colorful imported glass, Spode, fine dishes in many patterns, crystal, and silver pieces. Beyond these displays, the vast array of quilts on the wall formed a backdrop for more quilts layered on an antique four-poster bed. Mary, with the help of one of the women from the shop or occasionally a visitor, would put on white gloves, stand beside the bed, and tell the history of each quilt as they turned them back.[39] The "turning of the quilts," was repeated many times each day, as busloads of visitors, as many as 100 to 125 a day, came to the shop.[40]

Some of these quilts were from Mary's collection, but most were examples of quilts available to make or to purchase. After seeing "the turning of the quilts," quilters could purchase their next quilt in a variety of ways: paper patterns, stamped, ready cut, basted (if applique), or finished. Additional shelves displayed pillow covers showing both applique and pieced work. Wamsutta sheets and pillow cases plus a full line of quilt tools, patterns, templates, thread, and fabric were available.

Mary had established a successful family business. The McElwains had a lovely home in Walworth, where Mary entertained frequently with the help of a housekeeper, and a cottage at Lake Geneva in Fontana. They always had a recent model Buick car, which William loved to drive. The business was so well established that when Mary died in 1943, her daughter and husband (with the help of many dedicated employees and friends) continued to run the shop for fourteen years. Her daughter DeEtte died in June 1957, and a few months later William McElwain died. The McElwains' son-in-law, Jim Robars, continued the shop a few years longer, closing it in 1960. The shop had been in business for forty-eight years.[41]

Yet her legend lives on. Fourteen issues of *Quilter's Newsletter Magazine* from 1970 to 1985 have mentioned the shop, and twice her patterns have been featured on the cover. In the February 1971 issue, one reader, a pattern collector, wondered where she was. "What has happened to Mary McElwain," she asked.[42]

She enjoyed great popularity while she lived. Mary captured the interest of quiltmakers and satisfied their needs to make quality heirloom quilts. Her reputation lives on through the quilts she helped create. The shop, well-known in this country, sent quilts all over the world and achieved financial success through Mary's sound business practices during two World Wars and the Great Depression. The merchandising concepts that guided the shop continued even after her death in 1943. The shop continued for many successful years guided by her precepts and even today we read her catalog and wish *we* could stop by the Mary A. McElwain Quilt Shop in Walworth, Wisconsin, for a "turning of the quilts."

Acknowledgments

Pat L. Nickols and The American Quilt Study Group wish to thank the Canyon Quilters, San Diego, CA and the El Camino Quilters, Oceanside, CA for their generous contributions toward the publication of this paper.

Notes and References

1. Mary A. McElwain, *Romance of the Village Quilts* (Beloit, WI: The Daily News Pub. Co., 1936), 2.
2. "Celebrate Fiftieth Anniversary," *The Walworth Times*, November 7, 1940.
3. *Romance of The Village Quilts*.
4. Nettie Edington McElwain, "History Sheet of William Elliot McElwain and Mary Ann Alyger," typescript, (1951) collection of Virginia McElwain Hueschen.
5. Virginia McElwain Hueschen, interview with author, Walworth, WI, August 7, 1991, and correspondence, October 1990 to October 1991.
6. "Services Wednesday For W. E. McElwain, Lived Here 57 Years," *The Walworth Times*, October 7, 1957.
7. Hueschen interview.
8. Peg O'Brien, "Notables on Patron list of Walworth Quilt Maker," *Janesville (WI) Gazette*, May 31, 1930.
9. Mary Ellen McElwain Bryan, interview with author, Walworth, WI, August 7, 1991, and correspondence November 1990 to October 1991.
10. Cuesta Benberry, "Quilt Cottage Industries: A Chronicle," *Uncoverings 1986*, ed. Sally Garoutte (Mill Valley, CA: American Quilt Study Group, 1987),83–100; Helen Carbrey, interview with author (April to September 1991); Bryan interview; Harriet Alberth, interview with author, August 7, 1991.
11. "Mrs. McElwain Believes Busy Hands Make Life Happier," *The Sanborn (IA) Pioneer*, February 18, 1937, 1.
12. "Mary A. McElwain Quilt Shop Opens Attractive Studio," *The Walworth Times*, October 12, 1933:1
13. *The Walworth Times*, February 2, 1930; September 18, 1930; November 20, 1930; November 17, 1932.
14. Merikay Waldvogel, *Soft Covers For Hard Times: Quiltmaking & The Great Depression* (Nashville TN: Rutledge Hill, 1990), xi-xv.
15. "Quilts—Heirlooms of Tomorrow," *Hobbies—Magazine For Collectors* (January 1933):117–119.
16. Ruth W. Peterson, "Memories of Mary A. McElwain Quilt Shop," *Quilter's Journal* no. 24,(Fall 1985):17.
17. Jenny Furvor Neville (1869–1951) Collection, Grayslake, IL; Alta Neville, telephone interviews and correspondence with author, September 15, 1991 to October 1991; Arlene Neville Cole, interview with author, Los Angeles, CA, September 12, 1991 and correspondence October 1991; Robert

Mann, interview with author Cincinnati, OH, October 5, 1991; Margaret M. Bryne, interview with author, Los Angeles, CA September 12, 1991.

18. *Janesville (WI) Gazette*, August 20, 1933.
19. Charlotte Belland, interview with author, Walworth, WI, August 12, 1991, and correspondence September 1991.
20. "McElwain Quilt Shop to Exhibit In Chicago," *The Walworth Times*, March 30, 1933.
21. "Mrs. Mary A. McElwain Is Judge In Contest," *The Walworth Times*, June 8, 1933.
22. Waldvogel, xiv; Thomas K. Woodard and Blanche Greenstein, *Twentieth Century Quilts, 1900–1950* (New York: E. P. Dutton, 1988),24; Barbara Brackman, *Clues In The Calico*, (McLean, VA: EPM Publications, 1989), 32.
23. Margaret Schuldt, interview with Alyce Ryan, Walworth, WI, September 22, 1985; interview with author Walworth, WI, August 12, 1991, and correspondence February 26, 1986 to October 1991.
24. Betty Harriman Collection, St. Louis, MO, Suellen Meyer.
25. Rock River Cotton Company Collection, Rock County Historical Society, Janesville, WI; Mary McElwain letter to customer Marian Orr, January 11, 1935; in collection of Hazel A. Hynds.
26. Benberry; *Quilter's Journal* 4, no.1 (Spring 1981): cover,1,2,8,12; Lucille Taylor,"Heirlooms of Tomorrow," *The Iowan Magazine*, (Spring 1964), article in collection of Shirley McElderry.
27. Rosalind Webster Perry, interviews with author and correspondence, February 1989 to October 1991; Marie D. Webster, *Quilts, Their Story and How to Make Them*, (1915; reprint, Santa Barbara, CA: Practical Patchwork, 1990).
28. Patricia Almy, "National Quilting Association Annual Exhibit," *Nimble Needle Treasures*, 3 no.1 (March 1974):26.
29. Grace M. Swanson, interview with author, Hamilton, VA, September 26, 1991.
30. McElwain, *The Walworth Times*, June 8, 1933.
31. *Romance Of The Village Quilts*.
32. Robert Markiewitz, interview with author and correspondence March 1986 to October 1991.
33. Clara N. Cohn and Linda Cohn Freeman, interview with author Walworth, WI, August 12, 1991; Dorothy M. Fulton, interview with author and correspondence, October 1991.

34. *Quilter's Newsletter Magazine*, 132(May 1981): 8; 138 (January 1982):20; 141(April 1982): 4.
35. Rock River Cotton Company Collection.
36. Markiewitz interview.
37. Mary Kay Stiles MacDowell, letter to author, November 1991.
38. Markiewitz interview; Peter Coleman, President, Hearthside Quilts, Shelburne, VT, interview with author and correspondence March 1986 to October 1991; *Quilts By Boag*, catalog, Elgin, IL (ca.1935).
39. *Quilter's Newsletter Magazine* 73(November 1975): 13; Ashley letter.
40. Alta G. Neville, telephone interview, September 21, 1991.
41. Helen Carbrey, telephone interviews, February 1991 to October 1991.
42. *Quilter's Newsletter*, 5(March 1970): 10; 7(May 1970): cover, 6, 15; 16 (February 1970): 9; 29(March 1972): 15; 31 (May1972): cover, 2, 11; 48 (October 1973): 24; *Quilter's Newsletter Magazine*, 60 (October 1974): 13; 66 (April 1975): 14–15; 73 (November 1975): 3; 132 (May 1981): 8; 143 (June 1982): 28; 168 January 1985: 53; 177 (November/December 1985): 61.

Tradition and Art: Two Layers of Meaning in the Bloomington Quilters Guild

Clover Nolan Williams

> Every experience deeply felt in life needs to be passed along—whether it be through words or music, chiseled in stone, painted with a brush, or sewn with a needle—It is a way of reaching for immortality.
>
> Thomas Jefferson[1]

Introduction

Perhaps no handwork is more closely and consistently associated with the inner life of its maker than the quilt, and perhaps nothing defines the quilt more essentially than this connection. While a series of interviews with quilters from within a single guild produced no clear consensus as to the form or methods of "traditional" quilting, all were united in describing the quilt in terms of an empathic connection with its maker's life and emotions, her loved ones, and the quilt itself. Members of the Bloomington, Indiana quilters' guild knew what the traditional quilt should "feel" like, whether they liked that feeling or not. What mattered most to them about a quilt were thus not an agreed-upon set of physical characteristics, but the associations and functions reflected in its features. Similarly, even such broad cultural categories as *tradition* and *art* were more important as culturally affective categories, defined in terms of association and function, than they are as objective categories.

Clover Williams is a doctoral candidate in Folklore at the University of Indiana in Bloomington. Her research interests include gender, material culture, and the construction of identity. Folklore Institute, 504 N. Fess, Bloomington, IN, 47405.

Both in quilting literature, and in private conversations with many quilters, I have found a profound ambivalence towards the designation "art," which was sometimes associated with modernity. Art was explicitly contrasted with "tradition," or—tellingly—with "utility." While all quilters I spoke with were pleased by the recent social trend which recognizes their work as a creative, skilled artistic expression, and embraced the term "art" on that level, many were reluctant to consider themselves "artists."[2] In most cases, this reluctance did not seem to come from a lack of self-esteem, but from their impression that the validations of art are at odds with more "traditional" qualities through which they defined quilting on an affective, or emotional, level. For example, several quilters quipped that in order to make a quilt an "art quilt" one need only make sure the work is useless and unaffordable, qualities which contradict the utility and generosity which many consider integral to the quilt's true value.[3]

The tradition-identified quilters I spoke with were not uncomfortable with innovation, but with an aesthetic terminology which seems to set the greatest achievers apart from their communities and removes their works from daily use. These women usually favored descriptions which, while not abandoning the creative aspect of their work, highlight an aesthetic of integral utility and belonging within the community. In describing a dynamic between "art" and "tradition" in the quilting community, I thus do not mean to imply that the terms are mutually exclusive; that "tradition" is without creative innovation," or "art" without soul. Rather, these words have meanings and connotations that go beyond dictionary definitions. Many "traditional" and "art" quilters are using different media and vocabulary to express similar values. At the same time, associations about traditional and artistic quilting often correspond to associations about traditional and "new" womanhood, and they may be cherished or ignored on those grounds. In order to understand this dynamic, and each other, it is important to explore the interrelation in the way these terms are used by quilters of various orientations.

This paper represents a folklorist's exploration of the uneasy dynamic between tradition and art as affective categories within the

Bloomington Indiana quilting community. I first discuss "folkloristic" theories about modern folk groups and tradition. An explanation of my fieldwork and methods will include descriptions of the Bloomington Quilters Guild meetings and sewing groups, and an account of how the thesis of this paper developed. I will then discuss in more detail the various understandings of the term "tradition" by members of the Bloomington Quilters Guild, occasionally comparing these with a number of manifestly similar assertions made by folklore scholars.

While both folklore scholars and the quilters I worked with often understand tradition in terms of age and inheritance, what each group implies with those concepts varies. Quilters' definitions of their craft and its relation to tradition will be discussed, as will quilting's association with nurturing and other virtues commonly associated with womanhood. In this context, quilters' perceived differences between art and traditionally defined "utility" influence quilters' attitudes within this dynamic. Unconditional acceptance of the term "art" may or may not accompany an explicit rejection of traditional associations of the quilter within family and community relations: Some self-designated art quilters I interviewed spoke of elitist and separatist connotations of "art" being countered by the medium of quilting. Others saw traditional associations of quilting as oppressive to women, and were happy to reject them. In each case, the terms "art" and "tradition" were defined affectively, and referred to each woman's personal interpretation of cultural values. My conclusions include a call for further dialogue among quilters.

Folklore, the Folk, and Tradition

Folklore scholars were once almost exclusively concerned with regional and conservative subcultures. Now many folklorists accept Dundes' definition of the folk as "any group of people whatsoever who share at least one common factor," and his assumption that this factor should be one that contributes to common communication and outlook, and to a shared sense of group identity.[4] According to this definition, which omits clear distinctions among folk, popular, and elite cultures, each of us belongs to many overlapping folk groups, although the importance of these memberships varies with context. Many travelers know, for example, that a shared language or nationality is often considered the basis for a common bond only outside that language area or nation. Because of this recent concern with different contexts upon a single group or practice, many modern folklore scholars have attempted to articulate and analyze the relationship between general concepts and real people. My original study, for example, was an exploration of how modern-day quilters related the general term "tradition" to their particular work and to themselves.

Attention to the particular has both altered and awakened folklorists' theoretical concerns with tradition. Early definitions, though vague, had to do with time: Practices which had been passed down within a given culture for a long time, through channels—such as the spoken word—which had existed for a long time, were considered traditional. Although these literal criteria for tradition are still used by many folklorists, others have blurred the term's legitimacy by pointing out that what is considered tradition varies, is often not old within the culture that practices it, and may be consciously added to a repertoire of practices. To use an example from quilting scholarship, Virginia Gunn has demonstrated that what was identified as "colonial" in "the twentieth century's first quilt revival" had as much, and sometimes more, to do with the fashions of the day as they did with colonial styles.[5] And quilting magazines routinely exhort readers to create an heirloom, legacy, or tradition, projects which indicate that practical understandings of tradition have as much to do with the present and future as they do with the past. Nor are all time-honored practices considered traditional. Suellen Meyer has pointed out that machine quilting has been widely practiced for well over one hundred years, since the sewing machine came into common private usage. This is a much longer time than many patterns, print types, and color schemes have existed which are widely considered "traditional." Yet the use of a sewing machine is usually not considered traditional among most quilters.[6] Other theories, which consider all or most group activity "traditional," usually do not explicitly address the fact that people do not use the word to designate any group activity, but a quite specific and personalized set of associations.[7]

I therefore focussed my exploration of the real-life usage of tradition on quilters' personal associations with the term. The questionnaire (see Appendix) asked questions about what might make a quilt feel more, or less, traditional, and to what extent feelings about tradition affected the way respondents felt about the quilt. Jeannette Lasansky points out that "quilts and quiltmaking played important roles in not one or two but the repeated and ongoing colonial revivals" and have been "valued for their romantic and historical associations."[8] Because these and other personal associations are so frequently expressed by quilters, I felt that they would have some very enlightening things to say about the relationship between quilting, tradition, and feelings. But while the women I interviewed expressed sentimental associations with quilting's past, they placed a more consistent and direct emphasis on its utility, whether past, present, or merely potential. Many felt that this utility was essential to the quilt's traditional nature and introduced distinctions between traditional and art quilting on this criterion.

Though the questionnaire made no mention of the term "art," several respondents used the term in contrast with tradition, as did Sue Childes, who wrote that quilting had become less traditional as it "changed somewhat—into an art form." This understanding of tradition and art was evident from my first meeting with one of the more informal sewing groups within the guild. After stressing that innovation was a part of tradition, one woman added, "But some things are just so untraditional, they're not quilts anymore!" When I asked what those things were, she responded, "Well—[laugh]—they're art." This comment was met with smiles and nods by the group. When I asked what sorts of "untraditional" elements would make something no longer a quilt, several women answered. Their examples, including the use of wood or metal, and unusual shapes, all implied a reduction of the quilt's potential household function. Because most of these women own quilts which are kept on walls or in closets, and never used as bedcovers, I have assumed that theirs is not simply a practical, but also an aesthetic concern, centered on potential function.

Quilters on Time and Legacy in Tradition

An understanding of any category of culture requires that one consider what it means to those who participate in it. This doesn't mean that all members of a given group will have exactly the same set of opinions, but that difference will often be framed in terms of an understood set of associations. For example, though there are surely as many "types of quilters" as there are quilters, within the Bloomington Quilters' Guild at the time I began my research, there were three types of meetings: the official monthly meeting, and the "traditional" and "not so traditional" weekly sewing groups. Attendance at each of these expresses alliance to a distinct collective definition of quilting. I began my research by visiting each of these types of meetings.

At my first monthly meeting, I explained the purpose of my research. After this meeting, I was invited to come to each of the sewing groups. At each, I handed out questionnaires to be completed and mailed to me, explaining that while there may not be room on the questionnaire for a complete answer to each question, I hoped to be able to interview them at more length about these and other questions. At the bottom of each questionnaire, I asked that those willing to be interviewed write their telephone numbers, and indicate when they could be reached. Of thirty respondents, ten were available to be interviewed at length.[9] I found those interviews more enlightening than I could ever have expected, and I feel confident that the information I received warrants the conclusions I have drawn about this group. My own membership in the guild and active regular attendance at meetings support findings from these interviews.

At least half of the guild's over sixty members generally attend the monthly meetings in the basement of Bloomington North Central Church of Christ.[10] Members who have a creation to share with the group come early to lay their work out on one of many tables for others to see. The meeting begins with a half-hour "social period," during which members admire the work displayed, and swap squares of fabric which many bring for this purpose. After a very thorough, efficiently run business meeting dealing with such issues as finances, planning and delegation, and discussion of future programs, a special educational program is presented. At my first meeting, the program consisted of a presentation and discussion of new and little-known tools and gadgets for the quilter. At the April 1991 meeting, Kathleen McLary, textile curator and chair of the Indiana Quilt Registry project, spoke on the history of quiltmaking in Indiana, and allowed members to preview the upcoming IU Press book, *Quilts of Indiana*. Other meetings I attended included a discussion of ancient Roman mosaic patterns and their use as inspiration for quilt patterns, step-by-step introductions to "English piecing," the transfer of photographs onto fabric, marbleizing fabric, and a slide show and demonstration of embroidery techniques used in crazy quilting. In general, no sewing is done at the meetings themselves, unless as a part of the special program.

Either before or after the featured program (depending upon how long the featured program is expected to last), quilters are encouraged to display their most recently completed works before the group. "Ooohs," "aaahs," and more explicit appreciative comments greet even beginning efforts. Pictures are taken for the guild's records and the quilter is awarded a small, gold-toned safety pin to be worn on her name tag. The women are also encouraged during this period to share special fabrics or other quilting-related acquisitions and to discuss frustrations, accomplishments, and tricks of the trade with the group.

Monthly meetings, though always very social and usually a rollicking good time, seem to function primarily to encourage quilters to value themselves as specialists in modern society. Much emphasis is placed on education, and on liaisons with national and international organizations and techniques. Meetings are run crisply and efficiently, especially during the business portion, which even deals with such issues as the guild's public image. For example, during the business portion of the February 1991 meeting, president Judy Wagner reported receiving a number of inquiries from persons looking for professional quilters. She noted that to endorse quilters from outside the guild implied accepting responsibility for the quality of workmanship, while referring interested parties to guild members encouraged the perception that members were, "a bunch of little old ladies with nothing to do but sit around and quilt."

Official positions within the guild include a program director (at the time of this writing held jointly by two women), an official historian, and a newsletter editor, as well as president, vice-president, secretary, treasurer, and various committee leaders. In addition to these, another position, museum liaison, has been proposed for the upcoming elections. As much as possible, then, guild meetings function to allow members access to types of public and official validation which many feel they have often been denied in the past, and which have acquired ever more importance in modern times. Because of this, and because the large meetings serve as a counterbalance to the isolation many modern quilters feel, monthly meetings are very popular.[11]

In addition, a number of members with flexible schedules and the desire for more intimate "working" groups, have formed two distinct "sewing groups." These groups meet weekly on Tuesday and Wednesday mornings. These rotating meetings take place in the women's homes. Each woman brings an individual project to work on, usually "piecing" individual quilt blocks together, or quilting smaller, more portable pieces such as wall hangings or crib quilts. The Tuesday morning group has been dubbed "traditional," while the Wednesday morning group call themselves, "not-so-traditional." This is not an exclusive division: a member who considers herself traditional may choose to come to the Wednesday morning group if she happens to be busy on Tuesday. Nor is the division either clear-cut or heated, though it is very quickly felt. At my first monthly meeting, members from both groups approached and invited me to their meetings. I was made very welcome at both types of meeting, although at both I was questioned circumspectly by several members about my orientation towards traditional quilting, and members of both groups tactfully and appropriately hinted that I might "be more comfortable" if I brought something to work on the next time.

If I hadn't known in advance which groups were said to be more, and which less, traditional, I would have been hard-pressed to deduce this. Quilters bring a variety of projects to each group and the members' homes usually display a number of types of quilting, including "cheater cloths," geometric piecing, and other forms. It was, for example, at a "non-traditional" quilt meeting where I heard a member express her distaste for quilting using threads which contrasted with the fabric being stitched. She felt it looked too "wild." And Edith Lawson, a self-designated traditional quilter who hosts and attends Wednesday morning groups because of practical constraints, loves to experiment with different patterns, and with materials other than the traditional cotton. She proudly showed me, amidst a plethora of "traditional" patterns, a beautiful appliqued quilt reproduction which she had made of Picasso's "Flowers." Thus the quilter's self-designation as traditional or as an artist may have less to do with the types of quilting she herself engages in than with the values she identifies with.

In defining "tradition" and "art," members of the Bloomington Quilters' Guild used abstract terms and concepts, such as history and legacy, in ways which the folklorist would find familiar, but they showed very little consensus in designating formal requisites for either. While one quilter described representational designs as traditional and abstract geometric figures as more artistically modern, several other quilters described geometric designs within a square as epitomizing traditional form, and Mary Beaver explicitly cited representational designs ("You know, pictures of things . . . ") as an example of the modern.

If pattern doesn't clearly indicate tradition, neither does any other single factor, including how quilting skills and aesthetics are passed on. In her questionnaire, Virginia Miller defined tradition as, "to hand down ideas from one age to another orally or by example" and noted that quilting was traditional because "ideas were handed down" and "ladies who learned it from ancestors started it up again." Yet when interviewed, she asserted that quilt books were traditional because "the things they're reading from that book were taken from people who had done traditional quilting." Even the monthly guild meetings, at which no sewing was done, she considered a perpetuation of legacy: "It's like they say in the Bible, the older ladies should teach the younger girls, you know, what they need to do. And it's just that way. You sort of hand it down. . . . They're giving examples and showing. The new people that come in and don't know quite how to do something, why, they take it to someone who does and learn how to do it." Marlen Rust echoed these sentiments in the following exchange:

Marlen	It has so much to do with the people—and *how* it goes from one generation to the other.
Clover	So how would it go? Parents teaching?
Marlen	Well, that would certainly be the *old* way of passing it, but *today*, . . . well, this group of quilters—the Wednesday morning group—and then I watch on TV, and there are these, classes. . . .
Clover	But it's still traditional?
Marlen	Yeah. But that Wednesday gathering, yeah, that's important.

Other explanations of traditional legacy which allow for diverse methods of transmission included Donna Marcus "continuation of patterns, designs, techniques passed along either in person or print from a body of 'quiltlore' widely shared among the quilting women for generations."

In addition to patterns and means of transmission, specific technologies and materials were cited by several quilters as a feature of tradition. Many women used these as an example of what a "fanatic" would require. Sue Childes notes that, "many 'traditional' quilters would not even consider use of a machine—especially in quilting as even 'legal' morally." A number of informal conversations at monthly meetings confirm that while most quilters I spoke with allow for at least some use of modern technology, all are sure that other quilters would not. But a number of quilters, too, echo Marlen Rust in pointing out that even in earlier times, "people were *smart*—if they had labor-saving devices, they *used* them. . . . Machine quilting has been around long enough to, well certainly, to begin its own tradition." As mentioned earlier, an article by Suellen Meyer confirms that in the mid-nineteenth century, women of all classes often embellished quilts and other needlework with elaborately visible machine stitching. Even poorer families were influenced by this trend, since machines were often shared among several households when families could not afford one of their own.[12]

Finally, several women mentioned choice of fabrics as a measure of tradition. Cotton, wool, "scrap," and other "functional" materials were contrasted, implicitly or explicitly, with "the new materials or fibers of today" (Sue Childes), or "unusual fabrics or . . . non-fabrics." (Donna Marcus) And several women specifically mentioned the addition of metal to a quilt as both deplorable and nontraditional. Rosemary Trubitt, who enjoys playing the devil's advocate, pointed out the traditional associations of cotton fabrics, but then went on to point out that the silk "crazy quilts" of the last century prove that even nonfunctional fabrics (and the quilts made from them) enjoy a place in tradition. Still, Virginia Miller told me that when she had started buying fabrics instead of making quilts from "feed sacks, old dresses," or whatever could be found, "it kind of changed a little bit," and she "began to think of it more as art."

If pattern, technology, and material do not distinguish art and tradition, neither does the element of creativity, which quilters of both orientations stress. Rosemary Trubitt, who unreservedly considers herself an artist, finds novelty a prerequisite of tradition. She says that "the tradition is that the quilter uses basic materials in a novel way to create something uniquely hers," and adds that she appreciates "the amazing variety within set limits." Women on all points of the spectrum emphasize the same point. Traditionalists Edith Lawson, who referred to "going wild" with fabric, and Virginia Miller, who told me that "quilting is quilting no matter how modern the design or color combination," echoed these sentiments. Though the tendency of art quilters to stress tradition to me in their interviews, while tradition-identified quilters stress creativity, may be considered a largely corrective measure, the statements were consistent and sincere. Perhaps Marlen Rust's eloquent summation of the tension between form and freedom underlies the statements of the other quilters. She says, "there's an element of play in these decisions about what to do when. . . . And now as I say this about *play* and experiment, I think about tradition where, maybe those elements are part of tradition." Yet she, too, goes on to point out that some innovations "step over the line," beyond which they can no longer be considered quilts, yet may remain art. Thus while innovation and tradition are considered inseparable, the quilt's essence is defined by traditional nature, however that may be interpreted.

Tradition and Art as Metaphors of Affect

Just as there are differences of opinion as to the formal details of tradition within quilting, so, too, is there a consensus about what these details should mean. In interviews and conversations, articles and books, both for quilters and the general public, quilting is associated again and again with comfort and love. As Cooper and Buferd wrote, in an oral history which was to become "The Quilters," an effective and popular play,

> The quilts were a compendium of family history, each person symbolized by a bit of textile. In addition, . . . we began to understand the quilts as. . . coming directly out of the home, out of familial interactions. The quilt was a made for a member of the immediate family, for a close friend, or a dreamed-of mate . . . The best elements of teaching, . . . early and often loving instruction, tradition, discipline, planning, and completing a task, moral reinforcement. Quilting was a virtue.[13]

Linda Halpin, writing for *Traditional Quiltworks; the Pattern Magazine for the Creative Quilter*, voices a similar sentiment, exhorting quilters to sign their own works since "a quilt is really a portrait of the life of the quilter, painted in fabric. . . . Pass your legacy of memories to future generations—you are important, and your work deserves to be remembered."[14] Both texts affirm the quilt as reflecting the inner life of its maker. Both echo Mary Beaver, who told me that quilting is "a way of saying, 'I have been here on earth.'"

Yet the magazine article represents a slight shift in focus, from the quilt's receiver and use, to include its maker's self-portrait; and from the authority of the sentiment itself to include the authority of future "quilt historians" and their assignations of value. Both are valuable, but many quilters are hesitant about a shift of valuation which they feel may, in setting them above their communities as artists, deny what they themselves find worthy in their own works. Scholars of women's autobiographies have theorized that women see identity not as an "essential and inviolable self which . . . propels the narrative" but as a configuration formed through its "reference and relatedness to others."[15] To many, the quilt represents this necessary integration of self to family and community.

A story from Mary Beaver illustrates the metaphoric power of this integration. Mary told me that she had often admired stuffed animals that others made from old quilts, but had never been able to bring herself to cut a quilt. Finally she found a quilt which was in such bad condition that she felt she would have no trouble cutting it, and bought it expressly for that purpose. But when the time came she felt, she said, "like I was cutting up an old woman." She showed me the quilt, still intact, folded away in a closet.

In her book on embroidery, Roszika Parker shows that needlework has regularly been identified with the decorative, sequestered state of several centuries of upper-class womanhood. Yet quilting has regularly been identified with a very different image of womanhood. Both needlecrafts have long been appreciated for their beauty and artistry, though they have usually been considered inferior to academic arts. Both, too have represented feminine industry and propriety, as well as the expression of, and "desire for companionship, love, and closeness in the home."[16] But in the homes and work of quilters, no matter what their social status, the woman represented in her work was not helpless or extraneous to the family economy but one who worked hard and played an integral part in the maintenance of the household. A 1935 book written by Hall and Kretzinger considered "the practicability and usefulness of quilted things and the joy and pride of creating things for everyday use" incentives as compelling as "art" and "self-expression."[17] If, as Parker writes, upper-class embroidery and its maker "made a statement about the family's social aspirations,"[18] the quilter, whatever her social aspirations, stated rather different hopes in her work. These hopes include the "contribution to family economy,"[19] and Mary Beaver's "labor of love from one family member to another," which defines traditional quilting for many practitioners. This difference in priorities recalls the differences I feel many quilters allude to in distinguishing the traditional quilt from the art quilt.

Each quilter interviewed cited potential or actual utility as requisite to the traditional meaning of a quilt. This requirement is illustrated by the quip, repeated by traditional and art quilters alike in some variation, that in order to make an art quilt one need only make sure one's work is useless and over-priced. This piece of wisdom, neither entirely serious nor yet wholly in jest, seems a common one among the quilters I worked with: One need only allude to it to produce knowing smiles among guild members. The importance of utility to the very definition of quilting is supported by statements such as Marlen Rust's allusion to the quilt's "use as protection, warmth," Rosemary Trubitt's reference to the literal meaning of the word "comforter" and her added comment "they *touch* you," and Virginia Miller's explanation that when she was younger, folks "made quilts or comforters because they needed a cover and they couldn't afford to buy one." Despite differences of opinion, cited earlier, about what patterns, methods, and legacies typify this integrity, each of these women is expressing a similar sentiment about the quilt's meaning.

The intrinsic utility of the quilt, as well as its beauty, defines its traditional essence and value. Without this utility, many find the aesthetic dimension of the quilt an empty beauty. Marlen Rust speculated that without the promise of utility the quilt might be "no longer a quilt," and indicated throughout our interview that not just construction, but use, too, carried and created a quilt's meaning. Similarly, Mary Beaver told me the story of a friend of hers who at one time was forced to make quilts commercially. When asked by Mary how she could stand to sell what she had put so much of herself into, she replied, "I just make sure my son sleeps under each one at least once." The value inherent in utility is thus not merely practical or economical, but describes practicality and economy as they link lives and sentiments.

The quilt is "traditionally" made, too, from the fabric of life. While few of even the most tradition-identified quilters I spoke with had made quilts from old clothing, and none held this to be a requirement of the traditional quilt, Virginia Miller did remark that quilting had begun to seem less like history or tradition and more like art to her when she began to buy fabrics with which to quilt. Recalling her childhood, she told me that "they made quilts for different reasons then than they do now—they made them for cover and couldn't afford to go buy a blanket. And so they made them from whatever fabrics they had on hand. And now they make them for the beauty." Again, utility and beauty are not exclusive categories:

She spoke fondly of the pretty printed feed sacks her family had made into children's clothing and then quilts, and showed me a piece of feed sack which she'd kept and incorporated into a current project.

Other examples of quilts literally as well as figuratively representing the history of family life through the fabrics incorporated into them are abundant in quilt literature. One example from *The Quilters* shares the flavor of many others;

> It's so much fun to pick up these quilts and see everybody's dresses in it. Oh, there's one of mine when I was sixteen. Mother saved pieces from every dress she ever made for me; when I got older she gave them to me to make a quilt. In her day pieced tops were all made from a woman's scrap bag, and, at that, time, more often than not, the linings were other old worn-out quilts or blankets. We never wasted a bit of cloth. . . used it over and over until it wore out. Waste not want not.[20]

Compare this to the statement collected from a quilter by Barbara Kirschenblatt-Gimblett about the scrap bag: "Different ones of my family are always appearing from one of those bags." Kirschenblatt-Gimblett comments that the "recycling of materials is a common method of embedding tangible fragments of the past in an object that reviews and recaptures the experiences associated with those fragments."[21] For both speakers, a deep connection with the events and people in their lives is given tangible expression through the materials in their scrap quilts.

The action of collecting materials and making the quilt itself is also an act of integration of self with community. The exchange of scraps continues, mechanically altered by an altered social structure, yet carrying similar import. Where once scraps for the friendship or beggar's quilt were culled from a circle of immediate acquaintances, now organized guilds facilitate exchange. In addition, magazines including *Quilters Newsletter Magazine* and *Quilt Almanac* offer as a regular feature a "Quilted Trading Post," through which readers may exchange letters, pictures of their works, or fabric squares. The published letters of many of these women reflect the assumption that quilting itself creates a community. For them, this global village adaptation is a creative continuation of an older construction of community, and not a break with that past. Many women even use either guild membership, or the magazine "Trading Post" to exchange squares for a "Friendship Quilt."

Friendship quilts were traditionally made by a group of friends to commemorate an event, such as a marriage or leaving the area. Each friend or family member made and signed one square of the quilt, often including a personalized poem or endearment. The friendship quilt was, as Virginia Miller says, "like looking at a picture album. You think of them when you see that quilt. And it makes you, sometimes it makes you look at the pictures . . . and try to think when did this one pass away? Where are their children now?" Today, when strangers exchange blocks by mail, and entering guild members have the right to ask collaboration on one such project, the meaning of these quilts reflects modern changes in the way we understand community and communication. Today's meaning and tradition are more likely to be consciously invested in associations beyond the immediate environment. For whatever reason, and despite the very different social circumstances of most modern quilters from those of their predecessors, the quilt still evokes a sympathetic community with its maker which for many stands in opposition to the elevation of the artist in modern society.

Quilters and Art

The association of tradition with utility and its related distinction from art are neither necessary nor constant. Spokespersons for the aesthetic accurately claim that art has a vital function in society. Yet many of our associations deny the necessity of that function. In common parlance even among artists, the aesthetic function becomes more salient as utility wanes. Examples of this duality are abundant, both in folk arts scholarship and in the context of the quilting community. In a *New York Times* review of the Museum of American Folk Art's "Five Star Folk Art" exhibition, Rita Reif cites co-curator Jean Lipman as saying "that lowered standards in folk art are the result of at least two developments." The more serious of these two being "the influence of . . . folklorists who advance the view that the significance of folk art objects is in their social history, not in their aesthetic quality." For the quilter unable to separate social history and aesthetic quality, or unwilling to submit to standards of arbitration set by Mrs. Lipman, called the "doyenne of folk art collectors," the validation of a *New York Times* review of "Five Star Folk Art" is a mixed blessing at best.[22] Quilters who are uncomfortable with being considered "artists" are often rejecting these external judgements, and not creativity, beauty, or art quilters.

The attempt to attribute ambiguity about artist status to either poor workmanship or poor self-esteem on the part of the quilter surfaces occasionally, though usually not among quilters. Researchers note, sometimes with a hint of surprise, that, as Cooper and Buferd put it "it was no surprise to them that we were interested in their work."[23] Quilters often speak of family and community recognition of their works. Too, several members of the Bloomington Quilters Guild have had photographs of their work included in the publications of quilt-related groups. Such publications and national competitions impose an internal standard of artistry which quilters, for the most part, are inclined to accept. This standard represents a furtherance of the jury of peers which quilters have always embraced in contexts ranging from state fairs to the "challenges" of local businesses, to local recognition on the informal level that Barre Toelken refers to in writing that the central audience of quilters consists of other quilters.[24] Thus when judgment comes from within the quilter's community, a sense of community is not disrupted, but reinforced by the process of validation as art. It is at this level, still integrated with personal significance, that many quilters embrace the term "art."

Quilting magazines, films, and guild meetings are full of testimonies to the joy quilters feel composing their own works, and in contemplating the works of others. In terms recalling the most academic of artists, Virginia Miller told me enthusiastically that what she loves most about quilting is the creative process, "I just love to get my colors together and the design figured out," while Marlen Rust described the attraction of quilts which make her want to absorb the internal creative process of their makers. Indeed, if creativity and aesthetics alone defined art, there would probably be no ambivalence about the term. But as Sue Childes points out, over-adherence to self-imposed criteria of either "art" or "tradition" could cause a quilt to become formalized, and thus to lose the value lent through both heart and art. She values "creative use of designs, fabric and color—something of the mind of the person who created it, not just hours and hours of work with no heart in it when finished."

Recognition of quilting by art critics and academicians has done much to revitalize and revalidate quilting. As Warren Roberts discusses, there is a limited number of reasons for traditional crafts to survive into modern times. In the case of quilting, two of these, the quilt's status as a prestige item, and the revival of quilting as a hobby, have been directly influenced by another—quilting's recognition by the art world.[25] The successful "revival" of quilting's popularity and the sincerity of modern-day quilters towards their work contradict Susan Stewart's pronouncement that "to 'rescue' a creative form in this sense would necessarily be a means of killing it off."[26] But the values of academic art applied to folk forms do, as she indicates, often present differing standards of appreciation, causing a potential polarization of form and function. Barbara Rubin writes that such tensions between elite and "folk" art are difficult to resolve because they reflect a "deeper polarization" in our civilization.[27] Perhaps, though, the dynamic relation between art and tradition posed to quilters today is not polarized or mutually exclusive, but reflects part of the richness of options available to modern women.

As we have seen, many tradition-identified quilters who are uncomfortable with the term "art" still stress the creativity and artistry of their work. By distinguishing art from these qualities usually associated with it, they distance themselves from an aesthetic system which ignores the values through which they define themselves and their art. In different terms, most art-identified quilters expressed a similar wish to "break down" this separatism, to bring the beauty and meaning of utility to the values of formal art. This was often expressed implicitly, through art quilters' insistence on the traditional nature of their own experimentation. Donna Marcus, for example, wrote that "innovations arise directly from the standard repertoire." And consider Rosemary Trubitt's previously cited assertion that the tradition demands innovation. Sometimes, too, the philosophy is explicit, as was Marlen Rust's:

> I like this idea that it [i.e., tradition in quilting and quilt patterns] is *emerging*, that quilts have always been an art form and now we're dissolving this idea of fine art and handicrafts and I *like* dissolving that distinction.

Many tradition-identified quilters are interested in dissolving the same distinctions, as we have seen by Virginia Miller's enthusiastic recognition of all quilts as traditional, despite her own preference for stitching time-honored patterns and fabrics. We see this, too, in guild meetings, which celebrate creativity in whatever form it takes.

While all the quilters I spoke with recognized quilting as artistic, only one of the women in this study unreservedly embraced an aesthetic which placed art above function, and the artist above her community. Her comment on the distinction between the two reinforces the definitions and distinctions already drawn between the valuations lent by art, on the one hand, and tradition, or utility, on the other. Describing traditional quilters as "co-dependents," she explained that they were unable to find intrinsic value in themselves and their work, instead drawing satisfaction and a sense of self worth from their service to others. What she considered the hierarchical aesthetics of art were more self-affirming for her than traditional ways. Though rejecting these values in her own life, she, too, associates "traditional" quilting with traditional vehicles of expression and validation for women.

Conclusions and Implications

This study has a number of conclusions and implications for quilters and folklorists alike. It has become a commonplace in folklore studies of the past thirty years to assert that one cannot study folklore without a sense of its meaning in context. The Bloomington Quilters Guild reminds us all that context and meaning are not singular, but always consist of interrelated contexts and meanings.

My work also supports theories which suggest that genres cannot be separated from their "social and spiritual," uses as well as their physical features, and that "at the roots of each genre there is a distinct field of meaning" which addresses a distinct human need.[28] This includes not just expressive categories, such as quilting and embroidery, but larger cultural genres as well, including "art" and "tradition."

As they are used by quilters, the terms "art" and "tradition" question benefits conferred upon quilters by an academic system of bestowing honor. Certainly the Smithsonian Institution and Mrs. Lipman enliven the art with both their attentions and their money—only an independently wealthy quilter would reject that. But while some find satisfaction in this, others do not. For many quilters the problem lies not in the honors they are accorded by the art world, but in the price extracted, and in other honors which they feel they are thereby denied. By accepting outside standards of validation, traditionalists may lose the measure of self-determination that comes from judging their own works according to their own values. Many feel protective of the local and interpersonal validations that define quilting for them, and that they themselves cherish in their work.

Many quilters who hesitate to embrace the word "art" feel that art and artists are cherished primarily by being rescued from the wear and tear of daily life, revered but not familial. In contrast, their own ideals for themselves and their quilts embrace an aesthetic in which utility itself imbues an object and its maker with honor. They cherish most what is most integral to the fabric of daily life. In this role the quilt links lives and sentiments, and quilting is an act which integrates its maker with the community and values she has chosen. These values recall traditional images of womanhood and women's work, and are thus central to quilting's role in historical and sentimental revival.

Historical revival, as Alan Axelrod tells us, emerges "as a multifarious and often urgent response to social stress and crisis," and the range of quilters reflects the range of options available to women today. But tradition-identified quilters are not, as Axelrod also seems to suggest, "turning to the past" because they feel threatened by innovation or "forces of change."[29] Nor are art-identified quilters rejecting the past: Both groups are actively engaged in both creativity and legacy. Revivals are never simply a passive acceptance of the past, but an extension of the selective piecing together of a present which is basic to human intelligence. As Kathleen Stewart writes, positing continuity among the past, present, and future creates a frame for meaning.[30] Though various quilters may go about this differently, through different interpretations of art or different concepts of community, each determines for herself what values and meanings she finds meaningful, and layers them into her own life. This is an important similarity, and one which we can understand better by listening to each other, and to the meanings behind the words.

The last of these words belongs to Virginia Miller. She had told me that now that it was no longer a household necessity, quilting had begun to feel less traditional and more like art. So I asked whether she thought the two were different and she replied, "No, I don't think they're different, I think they're the same. They're the same; they just feel different."

Acknowledgments

I am grateful to the members of the Bloomington Quilters Guild for their comments and moral support, and especially wish to thank Mary Beaver, Sue Childes, Edith Lawson, Donna Marcus, Regina Moore, Virginia Miller, Marlen Rust, and Rosemary Trubitt. Several members of Anya Peterson-Royce's class on "Writing and an Academic Life" read an earlier version of this paper and offered helpful comments. My thanks to you all.

Appendix. Questionnaire on Quilting and Tradition in Modern Society

Name Age
Residence (City, State)
Where else have you lived?
Where, and from whom did you learn to quilt?
In general, do you consider quilting traditional?
Why or why not?
Are there ways in which one could make a quilt which would make it be nontraditional? Less traditional? (For example, "tying," use of a machine, or unusual colors or patterns)
What are some of these?

Are there aspects of some modern quilting which feel or appear traditional even though they might not be?
What are some of these?
What makes a quilt feel traditional to you?
Does tradition affect how you value a quilt?
Why or why not?
What other factors affect how you feel about a quilt?
Please give your personal definition of tradition.

Notes and References

1. Quoted in Texas Heritage Quilt Society, *Texas Quilts, Texas Treasures* (Paducah, KY: American Quilter's Society, 1986), 8.
2. Kristen M. Langellier's "Contemporary Quiltmaking in Maine: Re-fashioning Femininity" reveals a similar trend among Maine quiltmakers. See *Uncoverings 1990*, ed. Laurel Horton (San Francisco: American Quilt Study Group, 1991), 34.
3. Unless otherwise indicated, all quotes and references are from questionnaires and tape recorded interviews with members of the Bloomington (Indiana) Quilters Guild between September 1990 and October 1991.
4. Alan Dundes, "Who Are The Folk?" *Interpreting Folklore*, ed. Alan Dundes (Bloomington, IN: Indiana University Press, 1980), 24.
5. Virginia Gunn, "Quilt's For Milady's Boudoir," *Uncoverings 1989*, ed. Laurel Horton (San Francisco: American Quilt Study Group, 1990), 81–101.
6. Suellen Meyer, "Early Influences of the Sewing Machine and Visible Machine Stitching on Nineteenth-Century Quilts," *Uncoverings 1989*, ed. Laurel Horton (San Francisco: American Quilt Study Group, 1990), 47–48.
7. Sociologist Edward Shils, for example, states that a practice must be in its third generation of practice before it can be considered tradition. He does not, however, define a generation as a lifespan, but simply as a link in the chain of transmission. Thus a tradition might require only three people and three occasions. See, Edward Shils, *Tradition* (Chicago: University of Chicago Press, 1981), 15.
8. Jeannette Lasansky, "The Colonial Revival and Quilts 1864–1976," *Pieced By Mother; Symposium Papers*, ed. Jeannette Lasansky (Lewisburg, PA: Oral Traditions Project, 1988), 97–98, 103.
9. I did not consider it appropriate to ask the women about their educational or economic levels, and am personally unconvinced about the values of typing people in this way. But because of implicit assumptions about

time and legacy in relation to tradition, I did ask about age, length of time quilting, and how quilting was learned. I could find no correlation between any of these factors and how each quilter identified herself in relation to tradition, though it is possible that a larger sampling would reveal some pattern.

10. This represents membership as of Fall 1990. The guild has grown considerably since, topping 100 members in February of 1992.
11. Langellier points out that the guild she worked with similarly allowed women "to learn organizing and speaking skills characteristic of the public sphere without fear and without assuming male registers of speech-making." She also points out the social importance of quilting guilds. "Contemporary Quiltmaking," 48.
12. Meyer, 41–42.
13. Patricia Cooper and Norma Bradley Buferd, *The Quilters: Women and Domestic Art: An Oral History* (Garden City, NY: Anchor Press/ Doubleday, 1978), 17.
14. Linda Halpin, "Quiltmaking 101: Signing and Hanging Your Quilts," *Traditional Quiltworks: The Pattern Magazine for Creative Quilters*, Issue 13, (April/May 1991), 64.
15. Bella Brodzki and Celeste Schenck, introduction, *Life/Lines: Theorizing Women's Autobiography*, eds. Brodzki and Schenck (Ithaca, NY: Cornell University Press, 1988), 5, 9.
16. Roszika Parker, *The Subversive Stitch: Embroidery and the Making of the Feminine* (London: The Women's Press, 1984), 157.
17. Carrie A. Hall and Rose G. Kretsinger, *The Romance of the Patchwork Quilt in America* (New York: Bonanza Books, 1935), 259.
18. Parker, 159.
19. Ruth E. Finley, *Old Patchwork Quilts and the Women Who Made Them* (Philadelphia and London: J. B. Lippencott, 1929), 32.
20. Cooper and Buferd, 100.
21. Barbara Kirschenblatt-Gimblett, "Objects of Memory: Material Culture as Life Review," *Folk Groups and Folklore Genres: A Reader*, ed. Elliott Oring (Logan, UT: Utah State University Press, 1989), 333–34.
22. Rita Reif, "Five Star Folk Art," *New York Times*, (section 2, late edition, September 30, 1990): 40.
23. Cooper and Buferd, 18.
24. Barre Toelken, *The Dynamics of Folklore*, (Boston: Houghton Mifflin, 1979), 110.
25. Warren Roberts, *Viewpoints on Folklife: Looking at the Overlooked*, (Ann Arbor, MI: UMI Research Press, 1988), 61–62.

26. Susan Stewart, "Notes on Distressed Genres," *Journal of American Folklore* 104, no.411(Winter 1991): 7.
27. Barbara Rubin, "Aesthetic Ideology and Urban Design," *Common Places: Readings in American Vernacular Architecture*, eds. Dell Upton and John Michael Vlach (Athens, GA: University of Georgia Press), 484.
28. Dan Ben-Amos, Introduction, *Folklore Genres*, ed. Dan Ben-Amos (Austin: University of Texas Press, 1976), xxiv, xxvii.
29. Alan Axelrod, Introduction, *The Colonial Revival in America*, ed. Alan Axelrod (Winterthur, DE: W W Norton, 1985), ix-x.
30. Kathleen Stewart, "Nostalgia—A Polemic," *Cultural Anthropology* 3 (1988): 227.

Quiltmaking in Counties Antrim and Down: Some Preliminary Findings from the Ulster Quilt Survey

Valerie Wilson

The North of Ireland has long been associated with the manufacture of textiles, from the raising of flax to the spinning and weaving of cotton, linen, and wool; to the printing of cloth, and the fine white embroidery of international fame. Ulster, the most northerly of Ireland's four ancient provinces, also has a long and important heritage of patchwork and quilting which, until recently, was relatively unknown and unrecorded. As a result of work by the Ulster Folk and Transport Museum and the Ulster Quilt Survey important information is now available which sheds light not only on Ulster traditions but, by comparison, on quiltmaking traditions elsewhere in the English-speaking world.

The province of Ulster comprises the northern part of Ireland and consists of nine counties. (Figure 1) After the Act of Partition in 1921 six of the province's counties—Antrim, Armagh, Down, Fermanagh, Londonderry, and Tyrone were combined under the official title Northern Ireland, to be governed as part of the United Kingdom. The remaining Ulster counties of Cavan, Monaghan and Donegal then became part of the newly formed Irish Republic. While the Ulster Quilt Survey will record examples of patchwork in all nine counties of Ulster this paper presents some preliminary findings from the two east coast counties of Antrim and Down. (Figure 2)

Valerie Wilson is a graduate of the Art College, Belfast, now part of the University of Ulster, with a major in textile arts. She serves as Textile Assistant for the Ulster Folk and Transport Museum. 28 Huntingdale Manor, Ballyclare, Co. Antrim BT 39 9XZ, Northern Ireland.

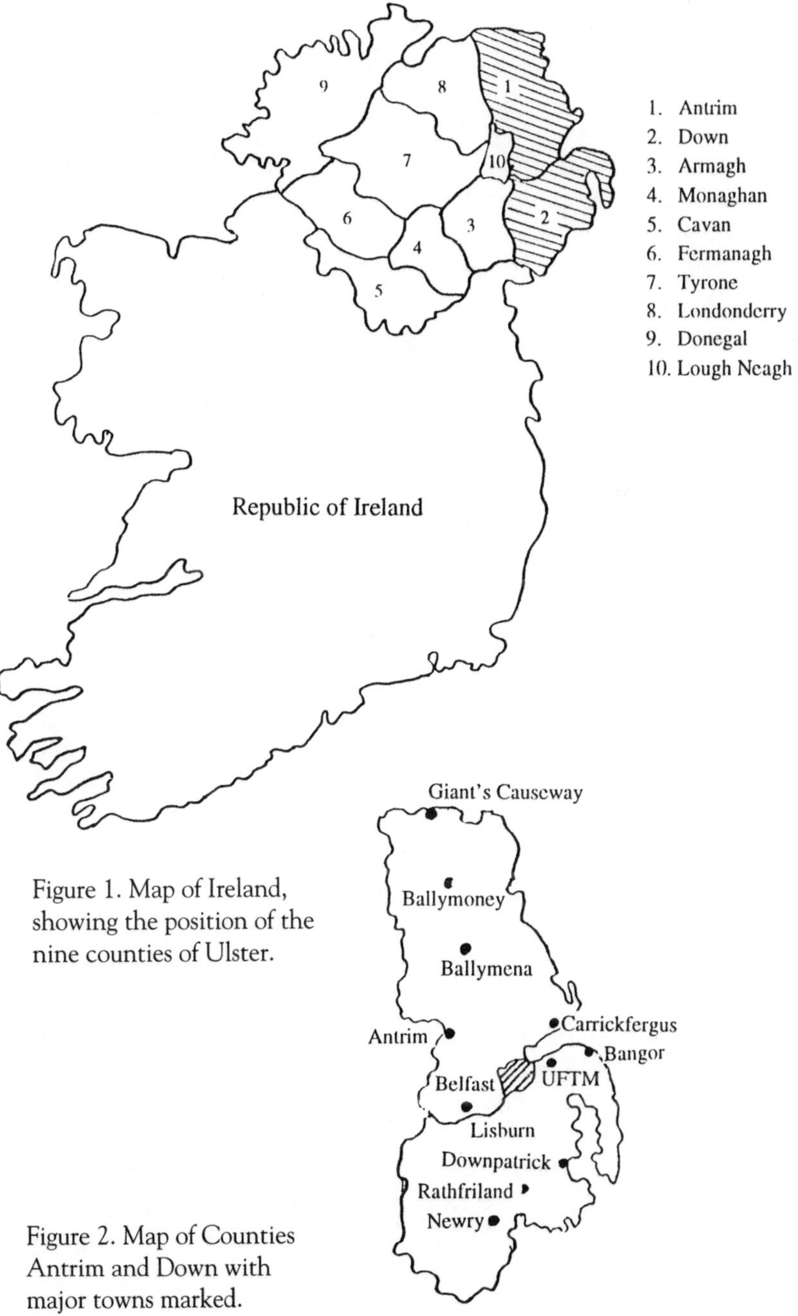

Figure 1. Map of Ireland, showing the position of the nine counties of Ulster.

Figure 2. Map of Counties Antrim and Down with major towns marked.

The counties of Antrim and Down meet at the mouth of Belfast Lough, where the capital of Northern Ireland is overlooked by the basalt plateau of Antrim, and they are joined along the route which leads to Lough Neagh, the largest lake in the British Isles. The sixty or so miles of the Antrim Coast Road, a huge mid-nineteenth century building project, skirt the foothills of the nine Glens of Antrim, leading many visitors to the Giant's Causeway, a spectacular formation of polygonal basalt columns at the Atlantic edge of the North Antrim coastline. From Belfast the coastline of Co. Down runs southwards linking tourist resorts and the many towns and villages of Ulster's east coast fishing industry. South Down is dominated by the Mourne Mountains, the highest range in Northeast Ireland.

The Ulster Folk and Transport Museum is situated at Cultra in Co. Down, seven miles south of Belfast on the shore of Belfast Lough, covering a site of approximately 130 acres. Established by an act of parliament in 1958, the Ulster Folk and Transport Museum now has the largest collection of quilts in the British Isles, with over 500 examples.[1] The collection was begun in the late 1950s initially to furnish the beds of the various house types reconstructed on site at Cultra. Fieldwork undertaken at this time by Katherine Harris, a member of the Ulster Folk and Transport Museum staff and a botanist by training, resulted in a number of exciting finds thanks largely to her understanding of quiltmaking as indigenous "folk art" worthy of scholarly study.[2] Having expanded rapidly from the 1960s as the result of fieldwork by successive curators the collection exists today as an important archive of a significant area of local textile history. During the 1970s the appointment of staff to demonstrate and teach traditional textile skills, including quilting, may be seen as an indication that much of the research at the time was focused on the interpretation of the collection in terms of the needlework techniques.[3]

In 1978 Alex Meldrum, a talented needlewoman from Co. Antrim and a recent graduate from an English College of Home Economics, was charged with the responsibility of assembling an exhibition of Irish patchwork for the Kilkenny Design Workshops.[4] This substantial exhibition, of some forty-eight examples of privately owned quilts from all parts of Ireland had a remarkable impact both in

Ireland and abroad and has been generally credited with the reawakening of interest in Irish quilts and the establishment of Irish quilt guilds. A short accompanying film, made by David Shaw-Smith for the "Hands" program on Radio Telefis Eireann has now become a standard teaching aid on the subject of Irish quiltmaking history.

Several years later, patchwork and quilted bedcovers were viewed in a wider context in the touring exhibition "Irish Bedcovers." This collection was the result of joint fieldwork by the Ulster Folk and Transport Museum, Muckross House Killarney, Monaghan County Museum, and the National Museum of Ireland in Dublin. In an exhibition of some thirty pieces, bedcovers were presented in terms of textile technique, e.g., knitted, woven, crochet, pieced, embroidered, and a full program of practical demonstrations was included at each venue. Specimens from the Ulster Folk and Transport Museum collection comprised the greater part of the exhibition and the accompanying catalog was compiled by Laura Jones, then curator of textiles at Cultra.[5] As an undergraduate I had benefited from Laura's knowledge of her collection, while I worked on a dissertation on the subject of Ulster patchwork.[6] Almost twelve years later, as a member of the textiles staff at the Ulster Folk and Transport Museum I was able to draw on this knowledge, plus subsequent fieldwork, for an exhibition in 1989 entitled "Quilts and Quiltmakers."[7] In setting each of the exhibits in the context of the makers life I had begun to appreciate the significance of the oral interview in research and the value of photographic evidence of quiltmaker's and their environment. By this time I was also aware of the various American state quilt projects and was following their progress with interest. I decided to begin a similar project and, after compiling a comprehensive questionnaire, launched the Ulster Quilt Survey in August 1990. Eventually all nine counties of the province of Ulster will be included with the results published in an illustrated publication planned for late 1994.

A core team of documentors has evolved, of historians and quilters, each of whose talents had added another dimension to the project.[8] We decided that, initially, at least, the selected venues would be those which already displayed and/or collected specimens of quilting and where there already existed some local documented examples

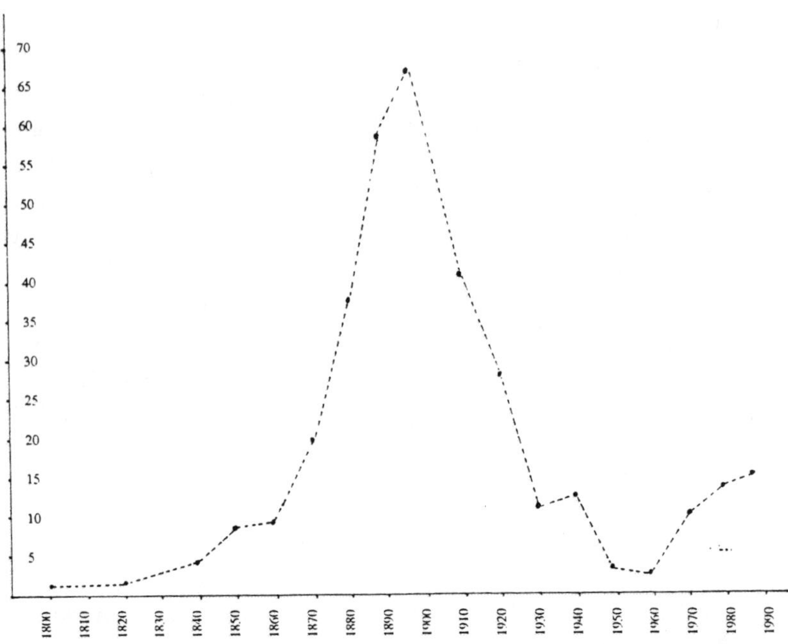

Figure 3. Chart showing number of quilts recorded so far by the survey.

of the craft. The first six venues have included museums, art centers and heritage sites. As the survey progresses smaller and more localized venues will be used as appropriate. There is no cutoff date for quilts recorded as it was felt that contemporary quiltmaking in the province has not yet been adequately documented. All of the quilts are recorded on 35mm color transparencies, and when the first stage of the project is complete, after the preliminary publication, these slides together with those already on file in the Ulster Folk and Transport Museum should form the basis of a sub-stantial quilt research archive.

Therefore I wish to present here some preliminary findings of the survey, illustrated with examples of particular interest, set in the context of general history of quiltmaking in Ulster. As most of the material available so far relates to the east of the province I have chosen to look specifically at the areas of counties Antrim and Down, and, for the purposes of this essay, have based my findings on quilt surveys in Carrickfergus, Lisburn, Ballymoney, Downpatrick, and a selection of provenanced quilts from the Ulster Folk and Transport Museum.

Of the 350 quilts in the study almost 65 percent are from Co. Antrim, the remainder from Co. Down. A breakdown of the dates of quilts recorded reveals a significant peak at the end of the nineteenth century and again, almost 100 years later as the result of a revival of interest in quiltmaking. (Figure 3) In terms of technique the largest group of quilts, 159, were those pieced either by machine stitching or hand sewing without templates. The next largest group was that of quilts pieced using templates—66, followed by applique—52, Log Cabin—28, wholecloth (including quilts made from printed patchwork or "cheater" cloth)—17, signature (autograph) quilts—11, crazy—8, and 9 quilts which made use of two or more of these techniques together in more or less equal proportions. The Medallion and Frame style of bedcover, i.e., one with a pieced or appliqued center panel surrounded by successive strips or pieced borders appears to be the most common and has been noted in almost 35 percent of all the quilts surveyed. This style was noted frequently up until the late nineteenth century, when block piecing and overall mosaic patterns (each accounting for approximately 25 percent of quilt styles) appear to have become more popular. The medallion and frame style, however, makes a comeback after 1910 continuing up into the 1950s in a slightly less formal arrangement. The next largest arrangement of pattern included those in stripform, around 10 percent, with the remainder covering a range of styles in a few examples of each. By far the most popular of pieced patterns was the Irish Chain, followed by pieced Hexagons, with appliqued quilts and Log Cabin forming the next most sizeable pattern groups. Of the Log Cabin quilts most were pieced in the arrangement known as "Light and Dark" or "Sunshine and Shadow," with additional examples of "Barn Raising" and "Straight Furrow". The "Pineapple" arrangement of pattern was noted in only a few examples, due perhaps to its apparent complexity. One red and white quilt of this pattern from north Co. Antrim (ca. 1900), was known to the maker as "Soldiers Wreath."[9] The survey was not just concerned with the quilts themselves but also how they fit in with the lives of the people who made and used them. For this reason "given" names of quilt patterns were recorded along with standard naming of patterns. Laundry practices with regard to quilts and methods of bleaching flour bags (feed sacks) were also noted, as was availability of sewing machines and the source of fabrics for quiltmaking. Some significant changes have taken place in Ulster quiltmaking over time, and I will attempt to describe those changes here with reference to Ulster textile history. For the purpose of this paper I will address these changes in five, clearly defined, periods of time.

1800–1850s (15 quilts)

As yet little is known of the origins of patchwork in Ulster and detailed research in this area is at an early stage. It has been suggested however that it was introduced here by the English aristocracy.[10] The similarity with the English piecing tradition of the late eighteenth/early nineteenth century and the predominance in Ulster of medallion and frame bedcovers with a central focus would lend some credence to this theory. In general quilts recorded in the survey, made pre-1860 tended to form two main style groups, as follows, Group A—Medallion and Frame, those with pieced, printed or embroidered center panels surrounded by mosaic pieced borders, and Group B—quilts pieced in an allover mosaic pattern or repeating geometric motifs.

Both of these styles of patchwork were widely practiced among the upper classes of England at this time, and there is some evidence to suggest that this type of meticulous needlework was considered suitable employment for the tenants on the estates of English gentry in Ulster in the early nineteenth century. An English visitor to the estate of Lord Mandeville of Tandragee, Co. Armagh in 1837, has recorded for us that among the many acquisitions on her trip was "a beautiful specimen of patchwork to exhibit, in the shape of a large counterpane, all made by the dear active little Irish fingers; with a dozen of handkerchiefs that might pass for French cambric, all grown, spun, woven and admirably made up, by the tenantry of this favoured nobleman."[11] Charlotte Elizabeth's roseate view of this venture was penned at the time when huge numbers of "active little Irish fingers" previously accustomed to plentiful work in the spinning and handweaving of linen, were having to turn to other textile skills in order to earn a living, following the introduction of mechanized spinning processes. The womenfolk of Co. Down in particular turned to the decorating of fine linens and cottons as an alternative source of income, with much of the work destined for agents in Scotland, through the important trade route between Donaghadee in Co. Down and Portpatrick in Scotland.

In the same period the cotton spinning industry, established in Belfast in the late eighteenth century had well and truly taken hold and the ensuing fifty years had led to a burgeoning trade in the spinning, weaving, and printing of cotton, with the raw fiber imported in large quantities from the United States through the ports of Dublin and Belfast. Hand block-printing of cotton was rapidly being superseded by faster mechanized processes leading to an even wider range of printed cloth available in local drapers and haberdashers.[12]

Three bedcovers from the survey illustrate typical features from this period and coincidentally are also examples of quiltmakers dating their own work, a practice noted in only a handful of quilts. The earliest is a mosaic cover, pieced by hand, of hexagon rosettes of delicate sprigged and striped cottons.[13] Embroidered in cross-stitch on one corner of the reverse side are the name of Mary Finyon and the date 1808. The bedcover is backed with white linen, a fabric which appears in several of the pre-1860 quilts either as backing or as the ground for an appliqued or embroidered center medallion. The earliest documented quilt in the Ulster Folk and Transport Museum collection is a magnificent corded quilt of white linen, believed to have been made in Bessbrook, Co. Armagh in 1790. In general though, linen does not feature as largely in quilts as one might expect, and, to date, no quilt of all linen composition has been recorded by the survey.

In a second example the maker, Susan Craig, originally of Co. Armagh, has marked her maiden name and the date 1820, in ink, above a floral printed chintz panel. This panel, centrally placed, is typical of those produced in the early nineteenth century for use in home furnishings and is here surrounded by pieced borders of cotton prints.[14] The backing is of white cotton. On the top lefthand corner is marked "Susan and Robert Johnson 1834" indicating their wedding date. The earlier date perhaps refers to the completion of the quilt. This bedcover was subsequently used in the family home near Lisburn, county Antrim and is now highly prized by the present owner, Susan Johnson's great-great-granddaughter.

The third signed example, from Ardglass, Co. Down, contains an elaborate central panel of floral embroidery in wool on linen, surrounded by a network of mosaic-pieced Irish Chain patchwork in blue and white featuring over twenty different cotton prints.[15] In the center panel the numbers "5.81" are marked in ink and the initials "M + G" are intertwined in wool embroidery. The numbers are most likely a shorthand date, and the initials may refer to the surname of the likely maker, a Miss McConvey, and that of her husband, Mr. Gilchrist. Little else is known of this quilt's background, but it would appear to be a fine example of a "marriage" quilt.

A common feature of these early examples is the presence of what is known as "wave" quilting. In over eighty percent of the bedcovers in this study the handquilting pattern most often employed was that of a series of chevron lines worked a half-inch/three-quarter-inch apart, known as "waves." (Figure 4) The survey has shown that this practice is constant from the early nineteenth century up until about 1920 when it appears to have been almost universally abandoned in favour of machine quilting in a grid pattern of diamonds on parallel lines.

Another important feature common to these quilts is the absence of wadding. Most Ulster bedcovers consist of a top and backing layer stitched together without wadding. Of the two crafts the piecing of fabrics was considered more important in Ulster with quilting performing only the functional role of holding the fabrics together securely. A few exceptions to this rule exist, but they are rare. Where a central layer or wadding has been used it is often a worn wool blanket or the remains of a previous bedcover.

The dominance, throughout the nineteenth century, of mosaic piecing (i.e., handpiecing of geometric template shapes) and "wave" quilting is perhaps less surprising when viewed in the context of needlework as taught in the National School System in Ireland. In

Figure 4. Quilting in the "wave" pattern, on a frame, as demonstrated by quilter Mrs. Mullan of Lisnaskea, Co. Fermanagh, 1974.

1814, the Kildare Place Society founded an establishment for the training of teachers in a variety of skills, including needlework. In 1853, the Society published a needlework instruction book, which included details of how to sew template patchwork and "wave" quilting. A few of these school books survive today, complete with meticulously worked examples. These and other incomplete patchwork projects offer opportunities for close study of early nineteenth century skills and techniques.

1860–1890s (130 quilts)

This period marked some significant changes in quiltmaking in Co. Antrim and Down, not only in terms of the patterns and fabrics used but also in the increasing availability of sewing machines and the popularity of the sociable aspect of the craft, known as the "quilting party."

During this period, political upheaval in America caused the supply of raw cotton to Ireland to be interrupted and indirectly led to a resurgence of the linen industry, which was to benefit from the recent advances in mechanized spinning and weaving processes. The cotton printing industry survived this set-back, however, and with the increasing sophistication of engraved roller printing continued to provide large quantities of cloth both for the local market and beyond. In some instances the skills of the block printers had not been discarded entirely. In 1888, it was noted of the Dunmurray Printing and Finishing Works, "handkerchiefs, lawns, linens, unions and cottons are printed, hand and roller processes being used in combination. Finishing is done by beetling and other methods. About 100 people are constantly employed. Of the work turned out, the greater part goes to Belfast merchants for America, London and continental markets. The remainder to Lurgan, Ballymena [Co. Antrim] and Dromore [Co. Down]."[16]

The exact distribution of these printed cottons and a record of their textile designs is the subject for further research, but it would appear safe to assume that at least a proportion of these locally produced fabrics would have found their way into the hands of local drapers, tailors, and dressmakers, and thence into quilts.

The "country dressmaker" featured prominently in the survey, often employing her couturier skills and cloth remnants in quiltmaking. Many of the resulting quilts exist today as fabric scrap-books of the latter half of the nineteenth century. One of the finest of these quilts is a large medallion and frame bedcover in pink and lilac small-scale printed cottons, with a central panel of Broderie Perse-worked applique surrounded by a wide border of small hexagons.[17] It was made by a Co. Down dressmaker, Mary Anne McKelvey of Bally-nahinch prior to her marriage to Robert McCalla

Figure 5. Pieced and appliqued bedcover. Lilac print cottons and plain white cotton. Wave quilted. Made 1870 in Rathfriland, Co. Down, by Margaret Waterson. (UFTM collection).

in 1870. A study of costume from this period reveals the popularity of lilac and purple prints, which may be linked to etiquette in mourning dress at that time. An appliqued and pieced quilt believed to have been made by Margaret Waterson of Rathfriland, Co. Down, in 1870, contains at least 10 different lilac prints in an unusual bedcover depicting motifs from everyday life. (Figure 5)

The availability of a colorfast turkey red dye after 1870 strongly influenced almost five decades of pieced and appliqued bedcovers worked in red and white cottons. Among the pieced patterns, Irish Chain, Baskets, Log Cabin and Streak of Lightning were most popular. Among red and white applique designs one particular family of variations of a popular pattern stand out. These are sometimes referred to as the "Heart and Dove" or "Heart and Spade" pattern, although only one example of a truly recognizable "Heart and Dove" applique quilt is known at present.[18] (Figure 6) The others generally feature the motif in varying degrees of stylization, indicating perhaps that, unlike the block patterns which were made to an accepted formula, this was open to more individual interpretation. In all documented examples the technique has been the same: a piece of turkey red fabric, usually fine cotton twill, is folded into quarters or eighths with shapes cut out. The resulting distinctive snowflake-like shapes are then applied to the background as a complete piece of fabric with, usually, one large motif in the center surrounded by similar smaller ones. In most cases, after a narrow hem was turned under, the motif has been slipstitched into place, but occasionally fine herringbone or chain-stitch embroidery in contrasting white thread was used for decorative as well as practical purposes. In a few later examples purchased rickrack braid has been used to secure the edge. The maker of one Co. Antrim applique quilt, made about 1895, has left the viewer in no doubt as to the ownership, applying the name I. Dick (the I for Isabella) to the lower part of the bedcover in red braid letters about nine inches high.[19]

One of the finest of these red and white applique bedcovers was made about 1875 by a Co. Antrim woman, Ellen Parker.[20] Ellen lived at Ferniskey, near Kells with her husband and five children. (Figure 7) Their farm of around nine acres would have been considered moderately small for the time and provided for only a part of their income. To supplement their livelihood Ellen's husband Robert worked as a millwright. Robert Parker, in common with many other tradesmen of the day, had to travel to find work, so much of the day-to-day running of the farm was left to Ellen. Around this she managed to find time for quiltmaking and the Folk Museum now has nine bedcovers from this family, some made by Ellen, others made by her daughter. (Figure 8)

Figure 6. Quilt of handsewn applique in "Heart and Dove" pattern. Green cotton on white cotton background. Wave quilted. Believed to have been made in Templepatrick area of Co. Antrim, ca. 1880. (UFTM collection).

A further example of Ellen Parker's applique skills and use of turkey red cotton can be seen in a bedcover of repeating block units worked in a tulip pattern of lilac, yellowsprigged cottons, with leaves and stems of turkey red. This quilt, in daily use until 1960, was reputedly referred to as the "American" quilt as the pattern had been sent back to Ellen by an aunt who had emigrated to Philadelphia some forty years earlier.[21] The whole area of Irish-American quilting links is at an embryonic stage and is the subject of some current research by members of the survey team.

Figure 7. Ellen Parker, quiltmaker of Ferniskey, Co. Antrim, pictured outside her family home, ca. 1910.

Figure 8. Quilt appliqued in pattern known as "Heart and Dove" or "Heart and Spade." Turkey red cotton on white cotton background. Wave quilted. Made by Ellen Parker of Ferniskey, Co. Antrim, ca. 1880.

As previously noted the two-color combination of red and white was also popular for many pieced quilts, particularly those made prior to marriage. The documentation of almost thirty quilts known to have been made specifically for use after marriage attests to the Ulster practice of gathering up household linens, including patchwork for one's "bottom drawer." The "bottom drawer" quilt was Ulster's equivalent of the American hope chest quilts or the English "dowry" or "dower" quilts, and may have, quite literally, been stored in the lower drawer of a common piece of domestic furniture.

An Irish Chain bedcover, one of several made by Eliza Anne McKeag, Ballyhay Co. Down, prior to her marriage in 1873, exhibits some of the ingredients of a bottom drawer quilt of this period, i.e., a block pattern worked in plain red and white cotton. In this case the initials "E.A.McK." are marked in ink on the reverse side.[22] Simple patterns such as Irish Chain and Baskets were especially popular and, with wave quilting, lent themselves to group work, particularly in the finishing.

The completion of a bedcover, particularly a "bottom drawer" one, was often the occasion for a sociable get-together and this was known throughout Ulster variously as "the quiltin," "the chirn," or "the join," the latter two terms also used in connection with agricultural activities. The most popular time of year for a "quilting" would appear to have been around or after harvest time when fervent activity in the fields would lessen slightly and the fruitfulness of the crop celebrated in fitting fashion. The Ordnance Survey Memoir for the Parish of Islandmagee, Co. Antrim, in 1840, by James Boyle contains an early reference to one such event.

> Their harvest homes, or "churns" are still sustained with mirth and at their "quiltings" the amusements commencing about the middle of the day terminate in dancing which is kept up until an early hour in the ensuing morning.[23]

An important aspect of these events was the provision of food, drink, and of course entertainment in return for assistance with the needlework. The range of foods might have varied a little depending on the means of the household but usually included a range of baked breads, with perhaps potato-apple cakes, or a milk pudding. One informant lists the fare on offer at a quilting in the Glenavy area of Co. Antrim as "a bannock or two, a wedge of churned butter, a whack of cheese, plenty of eggs both hen and duck, a keg of the best." It would also appear that a dish called "sowings," made from oatmeal steeped and thickened into a jelly-like substance, was also occasionally served.[24]

The participation of men at these events appears to have been threefold. Firstly on a practical level, to build and/or erect the quilting frame, secondly to provide the entertainment, usually in the form of rousing come-all-ye traditional ballads, story telling etc., and lastly but not least, to avail themselves of opportunities for courting. An article by Rose Emerson, entitled "Quilting" concludes a detailed account of a quilting in the Glens of Antrim with the following observation:

> When the quilting was finished and everything was shipshape again it was usual to have a Ceilidhe and a dance. Occasionally the night would end with the prospect of another quilting in the near future as two lucky people decided to "go in double harness." Then there was the custom of "tossing the quilt." The boys after many attempts, would "capture" a girl, roll her in the quilt and toss her to each other. It was always said that the girl thus tossed would be the next bride.[25]

While the survey heard firsthand accounts of quilting parties in two areas only, Ballinderry in Co. Antrim, and Downpatrick in Co. Down, numerous references were made to the practice, particularly in mid- and north Antrim. Although quilting frames were recalled in one form or another there would appear to be few examples surviving today. Those described were almost invariably made to the same format, i.e., four slats of a light-weight but strong wood, two measuring about six to seven feet in length, and two measuring between three and five feet. These were secured with bolts at the corners where they overlapped and the frame was then rested on four chairs of roughly equal height to allow quilting to begin.

In a largely rural community sociable activities such as quilting would have played an important role, particularly during the winter months, and the evidence suggests that quilting parties were as popular in Ulster as in the North of England and America. Although the practices of handpiecing and quilting survived into the twentieth century, the introduction of sewing machines in the late nineteenth century had a significant effect on quiltmaking in this period. Sewing machines were widely available throughout Ireland after 1870 and were recommended for use in the National School System in the late nineteenth century.[26] A receipt dated 1877 records for us the fact that Margaret McKee of Rathfriland, Co. Down, purchased a Singer sewing machine plus a quilter attachment, from a Belfast shop, for the princely sum of £5.9s.3d. Alas, no records exist of Margaret's needlework. An interesting feature of the late-nineteenth-century quilts was the number of hand pieced and quilted bedcovers with machine bound edgings and, closer to 1900, an increasing number of quilts handpieced but machine-quilted in simple grid or diamond patterns. It would appear that, as sewing machines became more available, the sociable aspects of quiltmaking were abandoned in favor of expediency. The survey recorded whether or not households owned a sewing machine and when they were acquired. Although a few machines had appeared in households by the turn of the century most seem to have been acquired around 1900–1910. The earlier machines were usually hand or treadle-operated but after the mid-1950s electric Singer models (many of them specially adapted from treadle machines) were most often mentioned.

The commercial output of linen reached its peak in the late nineteenth century with tens of thousands of men and women employed across the province in the bleaching, spinning, weaving, and embroidering of linen for export world-wide. Some measure of the scale of this industry may be gauged from the following account of the Belfast firm of J.N. Richardson, Sons & Owden Ltd. in 1888:

> Messrs. J.N. Richardson, Sons & Owden Ltd are large employers of labour in nearly all the Northern Counties of Ireland, directly and indirectly. Their spinning mills, weaving factories, bleach greens and beetle finishing works, are situated in Antrim, Armagh, and Down and provide occupation for over 7,000 people. There is a special department for embroidered cambric and linen handkerchiefs and this also has become successful by encouraging women in cottages throughout Ulster to persevere in cultivating proficiency in needlework. The weaving factories are in Down and Armagh. In the vicinity of Lisburn, at Glenmore (Co. Antrim) the bleach works are situated. They were started 130 years ago, and are said to be the most extensive in the world, turning out 10,000 miles of linen textile every year.[27]

Such was the demand for Irish linen during this period that the aforementioned firm, one of many, was required to have agencies in London, New York, Paris, Berlin, and Melbourne. The cultivation of proficiency in needlework was especially promoted in Co. Down, where many thousands of women supplemented the family income by embroidering locally produced linens. Many quiltmakers identified during the survey were credited by their families as also having a degree of skill in white embroidery, often used to decorate household linens or underwear for their own use. A collection of late nineteenth century textiles, now in the Ulster Folk and Transport Museum, from a single Co. Down household, includes three patchwork quilts, five embroidered samplers, and several embroidered night gowns, camisoles, etc., of white linen and cotton.

Heavier, richly colored furnishing fabrics, and wool, hitherto scarcely noted in the survey became more common in the period 1880–1900 mainly in Log Cabin quilts and crazy bedcovers. In general wool production in nineteenth century Ulster was small scale in comparison to the cotton and linen industries and was largely confined to servicing the needs of the local community. An account of the Old Green Woollen Mills of Ballymena, Co. Antrim, in 1888, includes this observation:

> The trade connection has been growing for some years, but the chief work done continues to be for the farmers, who send wool here through agencies established all over Ulster, to be manufactured into tweeds, friezes, serges, blankets, rugs, shawls, knitting yarns etc.[28]

Much of the woollen yarn produced in counties Antrim and Down was spun and woven in the home for the making of blankets, some of which, through time, would find their way into quilted bedcovers as wadding. Woollen Log Cabin quilts from this period generally fall into two groups. Those with center squares of red flannel and a proportion of bright or light colors combined with dark, generally indicating a quilt composed of the remnants of fabric from the entire household's clothing, and those of all drab colours. The second group usually indicates bedcovers made from tailors' sample books, hence the more limited palette. It was common practice at this time to utilize the fabrics in these sample books either in Log Cabin quilts, on in mosaic pieced bedcovers of simple stripe or brick pattern. The quiltmaking traditions of Scotland and Isle of Man contain many examples of Log Cabin patchwork and relate more closely to late nineteenth century Ulster quilts than do English or Welsh quilts of the same period.

The fad for crazy patchwork bedcovers, almost universal in the late 1800s, appears to have had a relatively short life-span in Ulster, with no examples noted, so far, either before 1888 or after 1900. In general they are all characterized by the same features: rich fab-

Figure 9. Market day, Lisburn, Co. Antrim, about 1915. Photograph by W. A. Green (UFTM collection). Among the stalls is one selling fabrics and simple pieced quilts.

rics, i.e., velvets, silks, brocades, and elaborate embroidery stitches and decorative edgings, such as bobbles, fringes, and ribbons. In this category the most notable differences are in the degree of needlework skill of the maker.

Embroidery and patchwork skills were generally combined to good effect in the signature (autograph) quilts of the same period. Red and white pieced patterns in squares or triangles were usually used with occasional combinations of red, green, and white and some early-twentieth-century examples of blue and white used together.

In general these signature quilts were made to raise funds for church projects, with the Presbyterians in particular seeming most in need of financial assistance. Schools too, benefited from these community projects. A signature quilt made for Connor Presbyterian Church, Co. Antrim, in 1896, has been pieced of red, green, and white in Irish Chain pattern, with extensive use of transfer embroidery motifs in flower, berry, and leaf motifs.

1900–1920s (131 quilts)

After the turn of the century, the textiles industry in Ulster continued to develop in a manner which was to have direct influence on the type of quilts produced in the first thirty or so years of the 1900s. On a small scale, an increasing number of dressmakers and drapers were making use of their offcuts to produce quilts for themselves, and occasionally for sale. An example of this is a striking Log Cabin quilt in Barn Raising pattern of rich silks, velvets, and corduroys pieced by a Mrs. Sully, who worked in a Belfast millinery establishment in 1900.[29] Those who did not dressmake commercially found their fabrics elsewhere, often from among their own clothing. Markets and fairs played an important role in the local community and were often a source for second-hand clothing, fabric remnants, and on occasion for quilts themselves. (Figure 9)

The existence of a sample book of cotton prints from the Belfast textile firm of Robert McBride (undated but probably 1905) offers an insight into the wide range of printed cottons available at the turn of the century. The hundred or so pages of the book each con-

Figure 10. Interior of farmhouse at Toome, Co. Antrim, ca. 1915. On the bed is a cover of printed patchwork, or "cheater" cloth, probably in red and white, the most popular colors for such cloth in Ulster. Photograph by W. A. Green (UFTM collection).

tain several examples of prints in vermiculite, geometric, and stylized floral designs, mostly in lightweight dress or blouse cottons. The collection of costumes and other textiles at Cultra provides more evidence of printed cottons as seen in sun-bonnets, bodices, aprons, blouses and dresses of the period.

As a record of the social history of Ireland in the early part of the century the collection of work by the Co. Down-born photographer, William Alfred Greer, in the archives of the Ulster Folk and Transport Museum is unparalleled. Green, born in Newry in 1870, travelled widely throughout the length and breadth of Ireland and, in doing so, recorded many aspects of everyday Ulster life, including an important series of photographs illustrating pre-industralized methods of linen production. His photographs of a Co. Antrim farming family of around 1915 are of particular interest, due to their costume content, and views of house interiors.[30] (Figure 10)

The eventual processing and marketing of grain provided one of the mainstays of Ulster quiltmaking, the flour bag. The flour bag (feed sack), in one form or another, either as a background for applique, component fabric of mosaic piecing (sometimes dyed), or quilt backing, appears in over a quarter of all the quilts included in this study. Most often it was used for backing quilts, with four bags unpicked, bleached, and rejoined, providing enough fabric for this purpose. Although many quilts in the period 1880–1900 contained flour bag fabric, it appeared most often in quilts made between 1900–1920, and to a lesser extent right into the 1950s.

Flour bags were widely available, either from household use or purchased from grocers' shops. As recently as the 1930s bread servers in the Newtownards/Comber area of Co. Down would sell bags from their vans, and one Belfast woman recently recalled:

> I remember my mother going, before the war you know, and buying flour bags from the Ormeau Bakery, just up the road. Tuesday was their day for selling them and you had to queue at a certain door to buy them. I think she paid about sixpence for half a dozen. Of course you had to boil them for ages to get rid of the oul [old] flour.[31]

Recipes for the bleaching of flour bags and other laundering practices have been recorded during the survey. Long soaking (up to three or four days) in a solution of washing soda followed by vigorous washing (The brand name soap "Preservene" was mentioned in a wide spread of locations.) seems to have been the preferred treatment, finishing with the fabric spread out in the sunlight or sharp frost. That the fabric survived this harsh treatment testifies to its durability. Frequently, however, bleaching recipes were only partially successful and the existence of several local mills can be charted on the back of many bedcovers. The fabric was also used for other things besides patchwork, including sheets, pillowcases, and items of adult's and childrens' clothing.

Garment making, and the manufacture of shirts in particular, has been an important part of Ulster textile history since the mid-nineteenth-century. The large shirtmaking factories founded in the 1870s expanded rapidly to meet the demand for their high quality products, so that by the early 1900s thousands of women across the province were employed in the stitching of shirts and pajamas. Factories were situated in Belfast, Ballymena, Whiteabbey, Newtownards, and other centers throughout the province. Those in Londonderry were, and still are, the greatest producers, and shirts made here were once advertised as being "Derry made by Derry maids." Many of the women employed in these factories were allowed to take home scraps at the end of the week and a large number of bedcovers exist today as a result of this thrifty practice. It was not uncommon for factories to provide sewing machines for outworkers to use in their own homes. Scraps left over could then be used to make up much needed bedding. A Belfast woman, Mrs. Castle, provided, in 1980, a graphic account of this practice, carried out at her home in Rowland Street in the east of the city.

> The rent in 1914 was 2s.11d a week (in 1974 it was 10s.0d. a week) and my father earned 18s.0d a week. This was reduced to 7s.6d a week outdoor relief when he went blind at the age of thirty-nine. To support the family my mother was employed as an out worker for Mr McClure of North Street making nightshirts for which she was paid 2s.6d. a dozen. She tried to make three dozen a week but had to work hard to reach this target. She had to collect and deliver the work and kept an old push chair (pram) for the purpose.[32]

An inventory of the furnishings at this address, for about 1920, lists the following in the front bedroom:

> Iron and brass double bed along window wall. Straw mattress, linen sheets. Feather pillows, linen pillowcases. Two white blankets. Patchwork bedcover made from scraps left from mother's sewing. White valance. Valance on fireplace. Lilac or blue/white striped or floral wallpaper. Clothes hung on back of door. Small items in the trunk under bed. Full length net curtains.[33]

The house, and others from the same row are now reconstructed in the outdoor section of the Folk and Transport Museum at Cultra. Bedcovers appropriate to this house, based on the previous information, are included.

The manufacture of household linens also provided remnants for quiltmaking as can be seen in a String pieced quilt of bright linen scraps made by a quilter from Broughshane around 1920. The fab-

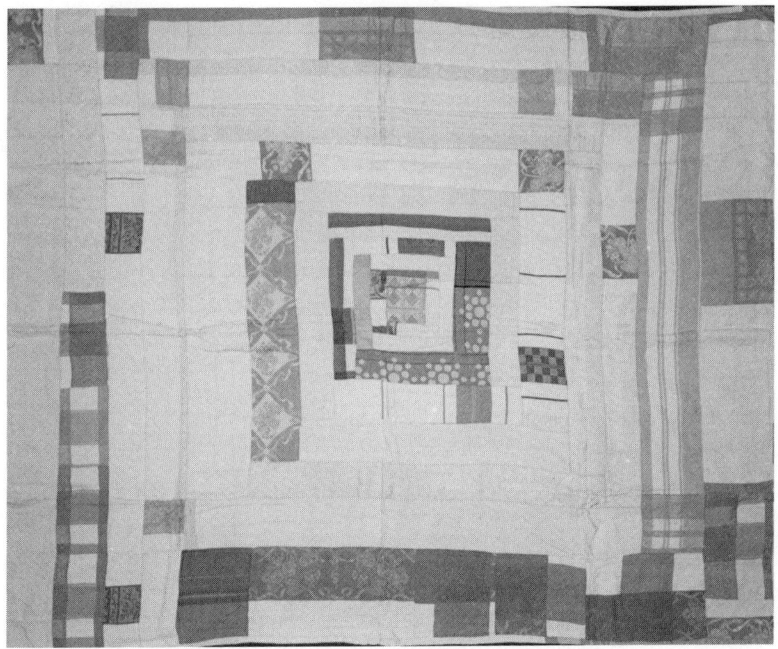

Figure 11. Quilt, machine pieced of tablecloth and napkin remnants in linen and cotton. Backed with flour bag fabric. Made at Belfast ca. 1910. (UFTM collection).

rics here came from a Co. Antrim factory where linen was bleached and dyed for the production of table cloths. A simple pieced bedcover, of colored damask table-cloth and napkin ends, from the same period sums up many of the characteristics of Ulster quilts at this time: simple piecing patterns, such as very basic arrangement of medallion and frame, strip, or brick, and use of factory remnants and flour bags. (Figure 11)

Traditional quilt patterns (i.e., Irish Chain, Baskets, Log Cabin) are not lost altogether in this period but were made in fewer numbers, and increasingly by machine. The revival of interest in quiltmaking in the North of England and, to a lesser extent, in Wales, did not occur in Ulster and, indeed, the 1920s marks the start of a period of decline for quiltmaking in the North of Ireland which was to last for several decades.

1930–1960s (33 quilts)

Of the thirty-three quilts recorded by the survey so far for this period, two-thirds were made in the pre-war years. Many of these have the same general characteristics of those made twenty or so years earlier, and the influence of the local textile trades can still be clearly identified. By this time many garment stitchers would have had their own sewing machines at home and would have made use of their skills to produce quilts for their own homes. For example, Elizabeth Magee of Ballymena was employed as a "finisher" (i.e., stitcher of finished goods) in the Braid Valley Spinning Mill when her father was spinning master there. Her paternal grandmother had a small draper's shop in Ballymena, providing a ready source of fine linen scraps. Several of Elizabeth Magee's quilts are now in the Ulster Folk and Transport Museum collection, including a Pineapple bedcover, machine-stitched in pale blue and white, and a range of small pieced sample blocks. Elizabeth's sample of "Rob Peter to Pay Paul" is one of the few Ulster examples of curved piecing.[34] A few quilts of this pattern exist, but in general curved piecing hardly features in Ulster quilting.

The years just before and just after the second World War are notable for a couple of reasons. Firstly, around this time some casual trade in quilts seems to have been quite common, born of necessity. Mrs. Magee's son, David Herbison, recalls that his mother knew of quilts for sale in Belfast about 1940, priced 10s.0d. each. Many of these were, like some of her own, made from bundles of scraps, bought by weight from local mills. At about this time, another Ballymena stitcher/dressmaker, Mary Carless ran a small but profitable sideline in simple pieced bedcovers, having an arrangement with her sister in Belfast who provided some of the fabrics in return for the occasional quilt top. Typical of Mary's quiltmaking in the late 1930s is a Triple Irish Chain quilt, machine-pieced of blue printed and plain white cottons.

A particular marketing technique for the sale of quilts was described to me recently by a Mrs. McWilliams of East Belfast. Mrs. McWilliams mother was employed at a Belfast Ropeworks firm during the 1930s and together with nine other female employees belonged to a quilting "club." None of the ten participants did any quiltmaking but each paid 6d. a week into the club account, for a period of ten weeks. A draw decided who received that week's quilt, and by the end of the ten weeks all participants had received, and paid for, a simple but wellmade cotton patchwork quilt. The bedcovers were made by a neighbour of one of the employees, in her home in East Belfast, and were often sought as wedding presents.

The second notable feature of quilts from this period is the reemergence of the flour bag as a staple fabric and the ingenious use of other materials, as shirtmaking factories switched for some time to the manufacture of uniforms and rationing took hold in the province. In one example, a Yo-Yo quilt (one of only two of this pattern recorded by the survey so far), made by Bridgid Hudson of Kilkeel, Co. Down, is composed of multicolored circles of printed cottons, linked together by a grid of dark yo-yo's, all cut from black-out fabric used as curtaining during the war years.[35]

In the 1950s, as the effects of rationing wore off, patchwork bedcovers, with their association of "make do and mend" were largely abandoned in favor of, successively, the "Alhambra" woven coverlet (a thick white cotton bedcover, commercially produced), the candlewick bedspread, and the ubiquitous nylon quilted cover.[36] Surviving quilts from the '50s and '60s are inclined to be bright, of florid colors, sometimes pieced of synthetic mix fabrics, and usually made in one of three forms: hexagon mosaic, crazy style, or randomly strip pieced.

In the mid- and late 1960s quiltmaking was encouraged in a small way through classes and exhibitions organized by local Women's Institute Groups and Young Farmers Clubs. In general though, this decade saw the least number of bedcovers recorded by the survey, and it would be another fifteen years before quiltmaking would once again emerge as a popular needlework craft.

1970–1990 (41 quilts)

Like other parts of the world Ulster began to experience renewed interest in quiltmaking in the late 1970s and early 1980s. The hugely successful Irish Patchwork exhibition assembled by Alex Meldrum in 1978 had a dramatic impact throughout Ireland and led indirectly to the establishment of Ireland's two major quilt guilds. In 1980, a group of seven quilt enthusiasts discovered, in the wake of the Irish Patchwork exhibition, that there was a need for like-minded enthusiasts to get together in order to learn techniques and pass on information about quilt history. During this year the Northern Ireland Patchwork Guild was founded, and in a short space of time its membership expanded to its present level of around 150.[37]

Since its formation the Northern Ireland Patchwork Guild has held its monthly meetings and annual exhibitions at Cultra. A recent development for this group has been the presentation of exhibitions in other parts of the province, sometimes jointly with the Irish Patchwork Society. This has resulted in some very successful shows and has encouraged the establishment of smaller quilting groups around the province. The inauguration of this guild happened at the time when American quilting books and magazines were becoming increasingly available in the British Isles.

A quilt made by a Northern Ireland Patchwork Guild member Anne Cardwell in 1981, serves as an accurate marker for this particular stage of the revival of quiltmaking in Ulster. It is block-pieced in a star pattern of pink and brown furnishing cottons with alternate blocks of plain white. The center wadding is of polyester, and it has been handquilted in a pattern of twisting cables, shells and flowers.[38] Superbly stitched, it exhibits all the hallmarks of quiltmaking as taught in the late 1970s and early 1980s in Ulster, ie., a mixture of "American" piecing and "English" quilting patterns. This quilt is now in the collection of the Ulster Folk and Transport Museum, and Anne's own written account of its making is very revealing. The following short extract gives us, among other things, information about pattern choice and availability of fabrics at the time:

> I joined several evening classes at Bangor Technical College and in January 1979 I enrolled for one term in the Patchwork class. I enjoyed it so much that I stayed in the class for six years. I joined the Patchwork Guild in the winter of 1980. My first quilt had been a Log Cabin design which was tied together but when the guild competition was announced I knew I wanted to quilt. It wasn't possible for me to have a frame so I chose a design that could be quilted in pieces and then assembled. The overall design of the quilt was taken from a picture in "American Quilts and How to Make Them" by Houck and Miller. The

> pink and brown fabrics are Dolly Mixture cotton curtain fabrics which are really too thick but at that time small prints were hard to get in local shops. I quilted all the sections separately with button thread and without a thimble which gave me a permanent hole in the end of my middle finger. I quilted my name and the date onto centre blocks. The whole quilt took from Christmas to May to complete.[39]

New quilts recorded by the survey, that is, those made after 1970, were almost exclusively of two types, either hexagon pieced or composed of sampler blocks. This appears to be a direct influence from local quilt teachers, many of whom in turn were influenced by American publications. Surprisingly perhaps, few of those engaged in making quilts now have any history of quiltmaking or quilt ownership in their family background.

Both the Northern Ireland Patchwork Guild and the Dublin-based Irish Patchwork Society maintain close links with the Quilters Guild, based in England, and some Ulster quilters are members of two, or indeed all three of these groups. Each of these organizations publishes a journal for members and holds regular exhibitions, sometimes on a specific theme. Contemporary Ulster quilters have of recent years contributed to international exhibitions and several have had work published in the British Isles and America. Visits to Ulster by leading quilt artists such as Michael James and Joen Wolfrom, in the past five years, have done much to inspire and educate, and led directly to the inauguration of a collection of contemporary textiles at Cultra, as a teaching resource. This collection includes pieces by Michael James, Joan Wolfrom, Pauline Burbidge, Lucy Goffin, and Richard Box, in addition to work by Irish textile artists Alison Erridge, Karen Fleming, and Alice Clark.

As opportunities for gallery exhibitions of historic quilts are infrequent in Ulster it is hardly surprising that few, if any, influences from the local traditions are being picked up and continued. By continuing with fieldwork and the collecting of specimens however, the Ulster Folk and Transport Museum fulfills a vital role in ensuring the preservation of Ulster quilting traditions.

Patchwork and quilting classes, for all age groups, held at Cultra, were introduced in the 1980s and are consistently booked to capacity. The houses of the outdoor museum provide the setting for practical demonstrations of needlework techniques, including mosaic piecing and wave quilting, and here visitors may also make comparative studies of authentic quilts in context.

The Ulster Quilt Survey has a role to play in documenting the skills of Ulster quiltmakers, past and present, and in helping to ensure the preservation of their handiwork for generations to come. In the 1930s a Co. Antrim poet, Mrs. Jane Curry, in a piece entitled "My Mothers Quilting Frame," reminisced about her mothers quilting days:

Upon her work you may discern
Unto this day a place
Where eager fingers sought to learn
The zigzag rows to trace,
Our small endeavours to destroy
Was not my mother's aim,
And she encouraged us to try
To use the quilting-frame.[40]

In February 1991, the blue-grey cotton wholecloth bedcover, wave-quilted, which inspired this poem was brought to Ballymoney by Jane Curry's daughter, to be recorded by the survey.

With a large number of quilts in the Ulster Folk and Transport Museum and a growing number documented by the survey, it is now becoming possible to form some sort of assessment of quiltmaking in Ulster for comparative study with English and American quilts of the same period. Some similarities, e.g., with early nineteenth-century English quilts, and Scottish Log Cabin quilts have already been mentioned. The most notable difference, however, between Irish, particularly Ulster, quilts and those elsewhere is the general lack of wadding, and the predominance of a single quilting pattern, that of "waves." The waves pattern was practiced to a certain extent in the North of England and the Isle of Man,[41] but not as exclusively as in Ulster. For the most part applique patterns in Ulster are either of the "Heart and Dove" genre detailed earlier in this essay, or of Tulip variations indicating a possible influence from America. Other possible American influences at play in Ulster quilts of the nineteenth century are reflected in a number of red, white, and green pieced or appliqued quilts and an increased number of block patterns towards the end of the century. Blue and white quilts are uncommon in Ulster, and the bright yellow or chromium fabric used in American pieced and appliqued designs is virtually unknown in Ireland.

Work on the survey is on-going, and further documentation will hopefully reveal even more data which will contribute to our knowledge of Ulster quiltmaking, and by extension to the history of quiltmaking generally. While Ulster quiltmaking shares some characteristics with British and American quilts, Ulster traditions are in some ways unique and the survey is continuing to explore these qualities.

Those bedcovers documented so far prove surely that quiltmaking, in all its forms, deserves to be viewed alongside the weaving and embroidering of fine white linens, as one of Ulster's foremost textile traditions.

Acknowledgments

The American Quilt Study Group wishes to thank the Northern Ireland Patchwork Guild for their generous donation toward the publication of Valerie Wilson's paper.

Notes and References

1. Ulster Folk Museum Act (Northern Ireland), 1958. 2.(1) "The Trustees shall for the purpose of illustrating the way of life, past and present, and the traditions of the people of Northern Ireland, establish, equip, maintain and administer a museum to be known as the Ulster Folk Museum."
2. Katherine Harris, "Patchwork and Applique Bed Covers," *Ulster Folk Life Journal* 21 (n.d.): 16–21.
3. Laura Jones, "Patchwork Bedcovers," *Ulster Folk Life Journal* 24 (1978): 31–47.
4. Alex Meldrum, "Irish Patchwork," (Kilkenny: Kilkenny Design Workshops, 1978).
5. Laura Jones, "Irish Bedcovers," exhibition catalog (Cultra: Ulster Folk and Transport Museum, 1981).

6. Valerie Henderson, "Patchwork and Quilting in Ulster and New England," unpublished undergraduate thesis, 1978.
7. Valerie Wilson, "Quilts and Quiltmakers," pamphlet accompanying exhibition, Ulster Folk and Transport Museum, 1989.
8. The documentation team includes Kenneth Anderson, head of the Ulster Folk and Transport Museum photographic dept.; Helen Rankin, historical research officer with Carrickfergus Borough Council; Cathy McClintock, a professional textile conservator; Francis Weir; Hugh Wilson; and myself. At each venue this core group is supplemented by local quilters and historians as necessary.
9. Ulster quilt survey ref no: BM/335.
10. Jones, "Patchwork Bedcovers," 32.
11. Charlotte Elizabeth, *Letters from Ireland*, (London: Seely and Burnside, 1837), 314–17.
12. D.J. Owen, *History of Belfast*, (Belfast: W & G Baird, 1921), 149–51.
13. Ulster Folk and Transport Museum specimen no. 387.1976. Part of a collection of textiles, donated from a moderately wealthy Belfast family, which also includes samplers and specimens of fine late-nineteenth-century costume and lace.
14. Janet Rae, *Quilts of the British Isles*, (London: Constable, 1987), 83.
15. Ulster quilt survey ref no: LM/153.
16. George Henry Bassett, *County Antrim Guide and Directory*, (Dublin: 1988), 151.
17. Ulster Folk and Transport Museum specimen no: 201.1988. At present the maker's great-great-granddaughter is, with assistance from three quilting friends, engaged in making a replica of this bedcover, using the needlework techniques of broderie perse, mosaic piecing, and "wave" quilting.
18. Ulster Folk and Transport Museum specimen no: 286.1974.
19. Ulster Folk and Transport Museum specimen no: 560.1974.
20. Ulster Folk and Transport Museum specimen no: 461.1974.
21. Ulster Folk and Transport Museum specimen no: 462.1974.
22. Ulster Folk and Transport Museum specimen no: 965.1979.
23. Ordnance Survey Memoirs for Co. Antrim. Public Record Office, Belfast.
24. From a questionnaire circulated in the mid 1970s by the Ulster Folk and Transport Museum, library archive UFTM.
25. Rose Emerson, "Quilting" *Glynns* 4. The Glens of Antrim Historical Society.
26. Advertisement for the Little Wanzer Sewing Machine in the official catalog for Dublin Exhibition of Arts, Industries and Manufacturers, 1872, as "recommended by the board of Nat. Ed. for Ireland for their 7000 schools."

27. George Henry Bassett, *County Antrim Guide and Directory*, (Dublin: 1888), 225.
28. Bassett, 323.
29. Ulster quilt survey ref no: LM/131.
30. T.K.Anderson, "William Alfred Green FRSAI: the Man and his Photographs," *Ulster Local Studies*, 13 no.2, (1991).
31. Mrs. Griffith, interview by author, Belfast, August 1991.
32. Ulster Folk and Transport Museum archive.
33. Ulster Folk and Transport Museum archive.
34. Ulster Folk and Transport Museum specimen no: 964.1978 A-F.
35. Ulster quilt survey ref no: KL/515.
36. Griffith interview.
37. Northern Ireland Patchwork Guild, *Ten Years On*, (Belfast: 1990).
38. Ulster Folk and Transport Museum specimen no: 273.1986.
39. Ulster Folk and Transport Museum archive.
40. Jane Curry, "My Mother's Quilting Frame," *Bells of the Heather* (Coleraine: Coleraine Printing Co., n.d.), 29.
41. Dorothy Osler, *Traditional British Quilts*, (London: Batsford, 1987), 116.

Hard Times and Home Crafts: The Economics of Contemporary Appalachian Quilting

Caryn M. Kendra

When Lyndon B. Johnson signed the Appalachian Regional Development Act in 1968, he declared to the fifteen million inhabitants of the coal mining areas that the War on Poverty had begun. In his address, President Johnson acknowledged the irony of the situation:

> Appalachia has natural advantages which might normally have been the base for a thriving industrial and commercial complex. Below its surface lie some of the nation's richest mineral deposits, including the seams which have provided almost two-thirds of the nation's coal supply. The region receives an annual rainfall substantially above the national average. More than three-fifths of the land is heavily forested. Its mountains offer some of the most beautiful landscapes in eastern America, readily lending themselves to tourism and recreation.[1]

But although Appalachia is one of the wealthiest regions in the United States in terms of natural resources, its inhabitants are among the poorest citizens in the country. A history of industrial exploitation has enriched coal and timber companies but has devastated the land and inhabitants of the mountain region. The mountain handicraft industry, which consists of individual crafters and small cooperatives, developed as one response to the situation. Crafts, such as quilting, woodcarving, and basketry now provide supplementary income to low-paid part-time jobs, unemployment, and social security checks.

Caryn M. Kendra graduated from Georgetown University in 1991 and plans to study alternative agriculture. 810 Washington Ave., Albany, CA 94706.

The impact of craft income upon an individual family is demonstrated by this West Virginia example. Chess Shrewsbury and Allie Blackenship were married in 1926 in Basin, West Virginia. Chess worked in the local coal mine at Stevenson, West Virginia, for forty years. They raised eight children; the youngest, Darla was retarded. Allie had learned to quilt from her mother when Allie was eighteen years old. She has been quilting ever since, more as a hobby than as a supplementary income. Today, it takes her two weeks to make a quilt. Between September 1989 and March 1990, she made thirteen quilts. It took less time when Darla, who died in 1965, helped her. Together, Darla, Allie, and Allie's younger sister Ollie made over 400 quilts in twenty-five years. Allie insists that her daughter Darla, despite her handicap, was a better quilter than she.

Allie started selling her quilts twenty-five years ago because she needed the money. (She was no longer receiving her daughter's monthly disability check.) Also, she just couldn't use all the quilts she was making. "I'd already given them away as gifts." In 1963, she charged $125 for each quilt. Now at age eighty-three, she has lowered her price to $100. Allie feels her work isn't good enough to sell. "They're just not like the way they used to be. I'm getting up there in age. And it's hard for me to tack them." Her granddaughter Billy mentioned, "It's her quilting that keeps her going. It gives her something to pass time."

Allie has won ribbons in state fairs for her work. "People come here, to Stevenson, to buy my quilts. They know me and my green house. "Once she was offered $800 for an award-winning quilt, but she refused the offer and wouldn't part with her masterpiece. Allie has lived alone since her husband passed away in 1971. Most of her family has grown and left the state, in search of a better life. But Allie, with her rosy cheeks, smiles fondly as she declares, "I built a home and I will stay here because it is everything I have. I don't want to live nowhere else."

The roots of the Appalachian economic problem date from the late nineteenth century. The growth of industries in the eastern United States created a demand for timber and coal. Between 1880 and 1900, speculators were busy buying and selling timber and minerals rights to companies and other speculators throughout the world.

They saw Appalachia as a source in the United States that could supply raw materials, cheap labor, and more profits for industrial production. The onset of World War I contributed to this market development.[2]

By the early 1920s, there were signs that the boom from World War I was subsiding and that economic hardship was looming on the horizon. The now fluctuating economy saw miners' wages rise as high as ten dollars a day during the wartime in 1915, and then spiral downwards to pre-coal industry wages during the Great Depression in the 1930s. By the end of the seesawing during the Depression, seventy-five percent of the persons living in eastern Kentucky, Southern Virginia, and West Virginia qualified for some type of government aid.[3]

Before the industrialization of the region, local residents relied primarily on local production and bartering to supply their needs. But the coal companies had fostered a change in the traditional agrarian culture making people dependent upon a frail system. When the coal companies no longer provided a living wage, mountain people were left to fend for themselves, without many of the independent skills of their forefathers.

The economic situation in the coal mining regions of Virginia, West Virginia, and Eastern Kentucky has never recovered from the boom/bust cycle of the early twentieth century. During the 1950s and 1960s, the region experienced severe economic depression; coal mining collapsed as a major employer.[4] By the 1960s over half a trillion dollars of raw wealth—coal, oil, gas, timber, valuable minerals, and cement rock—had been stripped and hauled away to refineries outside the region. This phenomenon left eighty-five percent of the Appalachian people unemployed and many families relying on welfare. Unemployment was three times the national average and the annual income was less than $3,000.[5]

An early movement to address the needs of mountain people drew from the European model of the settlement school.[6] First developed in London in 1884, the settlement idea spread quickly in the United States. Initially, the movement was very strong in urban renewal projects such as Jane Addam's Hull House in Chicago. In 1899, John P. Gavit proposed the idea of rural social settlements, stating "there needs to be now an evangelism to the socially and intellectually lost among the hills and valleys and on the prairies of this land."[7] The people who responded to Gavit's call for the most part were women from old, established families who valued public service. Many were academically trained at the prestigious women's colleges of Wellesley, Vassar, or Smith.[8]

In 1899, four women from the Kentucky Federation of Women's Clubs, feeling the urge to act on their social and moral responsibilities, went to Hazard, Kentucky, and set up Camp Cedar Grove. For six weeks, they ran a kindergarten; distributed magazines, books, and newspapers; and provided lessons in cooking, sewing, carpentry, basket making, and (later) weaving. In the autumn of 1902 with support from the local community, they opened the Log Cabin Settlement School with 190 students in attendance. This school was later renamed the Hindman Settlement School.

The missionaries were sincere and dedicated to educating mountain people, nursing the sick, caring for orphaned children, and assisting families in many ways. Jean Ritchie (a woman in the local community) reported that families moved closer to the settlements to be able to send their children to the schools. The women made a great impression on the people with their stylish clothes, the pretty furniture, and the nice way they talked. Jean Ritchie and her sisters were impressed: "What if I could grow up to be like that. It was like the whole world was opening up like a blossom"[9]

In addition to the self-esteem and community spirit fostered by these creations, settlement women realized that locally made crafts could be sold to contacts in the North, which would channel money back into the mountain region. Frances Goodrich, working in western North Carolina, published articles in mass-market publications such as the 1898 edition of *House Beautiful.*[10] Each article was accompanied by bright illustrations of mountain people busy at their handicraft work. Goodrich's efforts paid off. By 1904, the federal government, realizing the economic significance of handicrafts, got involved with the project. "The plan of supplying the materials and paying for the work on a piecework basis was adopted. For carding and spinning, the women were paid 33.5 cents per pound of wool or 44 cents per pound of cotton."[11] In 1908, Frances Goodrich opened the Allenstand Shop at the crossroads of the well-established livestock trading route between Greeneville, Tennessee, and Greenville, South Carolina. In 1917, the shop became Allanstand Industries, Inc. Shares were available at $25.00 each.[12] This was the beginning of "industries" promoting sales of handicrafts to markets outside the region.

The Industries Movement evolved into the Cooperative Movement during the post-Depression years. Cooperatives in the United States were modeled on the Rochdale Equitable Pioneer's Society founded in 1844 in England. Flannel weavers opened a cooperative store where they sold essential goods to members at a reduced price. The principles that evolved from the Rochdale experiment were open, democratic membership, limited interest on capital, patronage refunds, political nonpartisanship, constant education of members, and cooperation among other cooperatives.[13]

The cooperative movement has become an important part of Appalachian crafts marketing. Statistics from 1977 show that there are one hundred and fifteen craft co-ops in Appalachia, forty-eight of which are in Virginia, West Virginia, and eastern Kentucky. These institutions put great importance on self-help in times when outside resources are limited. For example, in 1977, a woman crafter of the Grassroots Craftsmen of Appalachia in Lost Creek, Kentucky, sold $2,400 worth of quilts a year, thus supplementing her husband's $150 a month Social Security check.[14]

Morris Fork Crafts is a nonprofit Appalachian handicraft cooperative in Booneville, Kentucky. It was formed in 1978 by area residents as a capital improvement project. The co-op's mission is to provide encouragement and support to its 110 community members who wish to make traditional mountain handicrafts and who live in the adjoining counties of Breathitt, Owsley, Lee, Clay, and Perry. Morris Fork Crafts accepts all homemade items on consignment. Liz Alden, a former volunteer-in-mission of the Presbyterian Church who worked at Morris Fork Crafts for nine months in 1989, explained the sale process as follows: "A quilter will bring us her craft complete with a suggested price. The quilt will then go before a quality control board to pass a routine inspection. After the quilt has been approved it is allowed to be sold. Eighty percent of each sale goes directly back to its maker and the other twenty percent goes to the co-op." This means that if a quilter makes five queen-size quilts per year, each of which sell for $550 at Morris Fork, she receives $440 for each quilt, a total of $2,200. Most crafters use this money to supplement other income.

Morris Fork Crafts participates in craft shows sponsored by Presbyterian churches nationwide as well as shows which are "specifically Appalachian crafts." According to Mary Finlayson, the present volunteer-in-mission at the co-op, "Surprisingly, the center sales are good. We are listed in the Kentucky Travelers Guide and calendar supplements in newspapers statewide. In these supplements we place an advertisement which is half paid for by the state. We also have a brochure in the state parks system, and being near two state parks means tour buses of craft seekers regularly pass through our center." Finlayson cited that it is possible to do $1,500 worth of sales in two hours when tour buses stop at the center. For the year May 1, 1991 to February 29, 1992, total sales for the co-op amounted to $79,089. This is broken down as follows: $13,772 at the store, $55,606 on the road at shows and churches, and $9,711 through the mail catalog and special orders. Total quilt sales amounted to $14,699 (Thirty-eight quilts were sold and four tops were quilted.). But even with such profits, after paying the crafters eighty percent of the selling prices, insufficient funds remain to cover operational costs. This creates a big challenge for Morris Fork Crafts and has left the co-op dependent on volunteer time and donations to keep the organization afloat.

Besides supplying local markets for mountain crafts, many craftworkers have followed the example of Frances Goodrich in seeking markets outside the region. An example of an Appalachian woman who is participating in this type of work is Sandi Garris Fagerty. She was born and raised in Pittsburgh, Pennsylvania. She attended Pennsylvania State University where she studied speech therapy. Shortly after graduating from college, she married and moved to Centre Hall, Pennsylvania, near State College. After the birth of her second child in 1979, she started working part-time at the local craft co-op, Village Crafts, making Log Cabin potholders and pillows and learning how to quilt. She worked at home so she could be with her children. When her third child was two in 1981, she was asked to be a designer at Village Crafts. Sandi worked two to three days a week for five years creating the pictures from which patterns for quilts were made. In addition to her design work, she also traveled to wholesale shows representing the co-op.

When her children started school, Sandi left Village Crafts and began her own full-time business at home. Her work includes both contemporary and traditional quilting. Her contemporary patterns are primarily landscape and abstract designs. People call her a "new-age quilter" since her patterns are quite different from traditional patchwork designs. She makes wall hangings, quilts, and table runners. Because she has carpal-tunnel syndrome, a repetitive stress injury to her wrist, she cannot quilt as much as she would like. On average, she quilts for three hours in the morning and three hours in the evening. She pieces by machine and quilts by hand, using a floor frame for larger pieces.

Her business has been extremely profitable compared to most mountain region quilters. She sells her quilts to two wholesale shops and attends approximately twelve craft fairs a year in Connecticut, New York, New Jersey, and Pennsylvania. In 1990, she grossed $52,000, but netted only $22,000 after expenses. Her prices range from $6.50 for a potholder to $850 for a king-size quilt. It is necessary for her to make one wallhanging a week, which she sells for $200, in order to meet her budget.

One result of increasing craft production to accommodate the market of middle- and upper-class people outside the region is that it influences the type of crafts produced by mountain locals. Crafters were forced to change their designs to accommodate the lifestyles of their clients. For example, even though the city folk enjoyed the "old-timey" design motifs, they did not identify with the way of life of the mountaineers, thus forcing a refinement of the crafts' abstract features. The demand was there for well-made home-crafted products, but it was part of a larger reshaping of mountain traditions. Throughout the work of missionaries and social workers, mountain people were indirectly being taught that they were to be one way at home and act another for the "outside." "Cherish your traditions, but mind your manners; affirm what you are, but groom yourself for social mobility; life in the mountains is wonderful, but its wonders must be shaped according to the vision of the great stereoscopic world beyond."[15] This subordinating system continues to prevail since the crafters are skilled enough to produce such works of art but dependent upon the income derived from sales.

While craft production is far from a perfect solution to Appalachia's economic problems, it is nonetheless an important source of income for many mountain people. Appalachian House is a non-profit organization which provides an outlet for various crafters and co-ops in the mountain region. It was founded in 1975 by John Potter and Father William Sangiovanni. The store, located in Darien, Connecticut, presently is operated by Winnie Dolan and A.C. O'Rourke. Appalachian House sells a variety of crafts, including quilts. The quilts in the store are the least profitable items, since they tend to be the more expensive goods. The quilts at Appalachian House range from $400 to $500, while at other stores in New England and in the Middle Atlantic region, prices range from $800 to $1,000.

When quilters, such as Emma Reese and Eva Scott of Vanceburg, Kentucky, complete quilts which they would like to sell, they mail the finished products to Appalachian House with a suggested wholesale price. Upon receipt, a check is sent back to them for the amount requested. Appalachian House then marks it up twenty-five percent and uses the mark-up difference to cover costs of operation. Dolan and O'Rourke often make recommendations as to the specifications, designs, and colors of quilts which they know would sell.

David Appalachian Crafts in David, Kentucky, is a non-profit program administered by the St. Vincent Mission. Most of the program's ninety members live in Floyd, McGoffin, Knott, Johnson, and Pike counties in eastern Kentucky. David Crafts designs all their own products and teaches the skills necessary to make the crafts. Consignment crafts are a very small percentage of their total inventory. The Board of Directors for the craft program inspects all products before they go on sale. An hourly labor wage, approximately minimum wage, is paid to all participating members every two weeks for the time they spend producing crafts. Quilts, for example, take one to two months to make, depending on the amount of time the quilters have each day to sew. They are sold in the store at $450 for double-size, $500 for queen-size, and $670 for king-size. All the prices reflect a thirty to thirty-five percent mark-up to cover overhead. Consignment items, after passing inspection, are placed for sale at the price asked by the crafter. When the item sells, the crafter receives the entire profit. According to Julie Johnson of David Crafts, a typical worker is a 65-year-old widow collecting $350 per month from social security. She makes eight queen-size quilts each year, receiving $350 per quilt for a total of $2,800 per year. Added to the $4,200 per year she receives in social security, her total gross annual income is $7,000.

According to Sharon Berger of David Crafts, seventy percent of the program's sales are from their wholesale, catalog, and craft show markets outside the county. Retail sales, which are highest in the summer, due to David Crafts' location near a popular state park and an outdoor theater, account for only thirty percent of sales. Knowledge of the craft program has been spread by the Kentucky Department of Arts and Crafts, various local magazine guides of the area, and a book titled *Handcrafting in Kentucky* by the former first lady of the state, Phyllis George Brown.

In 1965, Title I of the Appalachian Regional Development Act created an agency called the Appalachian Regional Commission (ARC), a joint federal/state organization designed to examine the economic and social problems plaguing the Appalachian mountain region. In 1973, the commission allocated $850,000 to examine the possibilities of designing tourist programs within the mountain states.[16] Tourist development is hardly a new concept in the southern mountains. As early as 1748, George Washington visited the White Sulphur healing springs in Berkeley Springs, Virginia (now West Virginia). Twenty-six years later, in 1774, a cabin was built near the springs serving as a rest station for those visiting the springs. The White Top Folk Festival, in southwest Virginia, was organized in 1931. White Top presented mountain artisans, primarily musicians, from their homes to audiences who traveled from eastern cities. In the 1932, the fair arena was enlarged to allow local handicrafts to be exhibited. According to one of the organizers, "Those New York and Richmond people . . . will snap up mountain handicraft if it is any good, you know."[17] In 1973 the ARC proposed the development of tourist sites such as Capon Springs and Cass Scenic Railroad, Virginia; Mount Rogers, Virginia; Carter Caves, Kentucky; and Pipestem State Park, West Virginia.

Resort and tourist development did not bring economic prosperity to the local people, as anticipated. For example, at Carter Caves, Kentucky, the average annual income for all jobs was $2,206 in 1966, and only eleven of the thirty-nine jobs created were permanent. At Greenbo Lake State Resort Park in Kentucky, only twelve out of one hundred jobs were permanent.[18] Similar statistics represent employment at the Breaks Interstate Park in Virginia and Kentucky, the Cass Scenic Railroad in Virginia, and the Pipestem State Park in West Virginia.

Environmentally, the programs were failures. Developers, with few restrictions placed on them, created severe environmental problems of erosion, siltation, and inadequate sewage treatment; strained the local water supply; and disturbed existing drainage patterns.

But perhaps the worst result of the tourist development was the image it perpetuated of the local people; the notion that the local folks are in such a sorry way that they just will not make it if they don't get our help. Outsiders to the region called the mountain people "mountain white," "ridge-runner," "hillbilly."[19] Richard Jackson, a resident of Banner Elk, in North Carolina, recalls two ladies from Florida complaining that mountain towns had some dirty and undesirable people in them.[20] Visitors are drawn to the mountains by stereotyped and idealized notions of mountain life and mountain people and frequently express dismay that reality does not meet their expectations. According to one folklorist living in the region, "People come here looking for log cabins, quilts, and banjos, and they are shocked to discover people here living in trailers, buying blankets, and listening to the radio."[21] The Appalachian craft industry depends upon the promotion of this stereotyped and inaccurate view. Moreover, because Appalachia is perceived as a rustic place, visitors expect to purchase craft items at bargain prices, so that mountain crafters often make less then their counterparts elsewhere.

Cora Vest is a quilter who depends upon her craft income. She was born on August 13, 1915, in Ezel, Kentucky, the only girl in a family of six boys. After she married, she and her husband moved to a hundred-acre tobacco farm. They raised six children, three girls and three boys, in addition to sixty-seven foster children. Cora has been quilting all her life. "I've been a'quiltin' since I've been seventeen." She learned to quilt from her mother by piecing on a nine patch. "I was to quilt the way she liked it and if not then she'd take it out and I'd have to try it again." It was only in 1972 that she began to sell her quilts consistently. The timing was significant: her husband had died eight years before, her savings were depleted, and she feared she would lose her small tobacco farm. So now Cora's quilting had a different meaning. The income from her baby quilts made it possible for her to keep her home. "It's the only way I got carpet put in my house." An average day would consist of quilting two hours in the early morning, working on the farm all day, and quilting up to five hours in the evening.

Thirteen years later, she still relies on quilt sales to supplement her $311 per month Social Security check. She must quilt one baby quilt a month, for which she charges $100. She is unable to farm the land anymore, so she has a renter tend the tobacco crop.

Although she used to quilt on a frame, she now pieces by hand and quilts on a hoop. Lately, due to her failing eyesight, she takes the top to a quilting machine where it will be quilted. "It bothers me that I can't quilt like I used to."

Today, twenty-five years after Johnson's proclamation, the problems of unemployment, inflation, and the unavailability of retail stores and services in poor, rural areas still persist. Appalachia is decisively one of the most economically depressed areas in the United States. The long tradition of disenfranchisement—abundant natural resources and wealth controlled by outside interests—have placed this region and its people in a situation still dependent on government assistance. Very little of the wealth from Appalachia's vast mineral resources has been returned to the people who inhabit this land. It is a no-win situation. Crafters need the extra income derived from their work since there are few other steady employers in these economically depressed areas. However, by selling their wares to those living outside the mountains they help perpetuate mythic images of Appalachia and images of themselves as an unchangeable people. Despite efforts to free themselves of this dysfunctional system, they are still struggling to be independent. Mountain quiltmakers and other craftworkers both depend upon and suffer from their role as the producers of "Appalachian crafts."

Acknowledgments

The American Quilt Study Group wishes to thank the Northern California Quilt Council and Winnie Dolan of Appalachian Volunteers for their generous donations toward the publication of Caryn Kendra's paper.

Notes and References

1. Helen Ginsburg, ed., *Poverty, Economics, and Society* (Lanham, MD: University Press of America, 1981), 223–24.
2. Ronald E. Eller, *Millers, Millhands and Mountaineers* (Knoxville: University of Tennessee Press, 1982), 128–224.
3. Laurel Shackelford and Bill Weinberg, eds., *Our Appalachia* (New York: Hill and Wang, 1977), 245.
4. *Ibid.*, 297–300.
5. Alfred Allan Lewis, *The Mountain Artisans Quilting Book* (New York: MacMillan, 1973), 33.
6. David E. Whisnant, *All That's Native and Fine* (Chapel Hill: University of North Carolina Press, 1983) 21–23.
7. *Ibid.*, 23.
8. Frances Louisa Goodrich, *Mountain Homespun* with Introduction by Jan Davidson (Knoxville: University of Tennessee Press, 1989), 6.
9. Linda Johnson, Sue Easterling Koback, and Helen Matthews Lewis, "Family, Religion, and Colonialism in Central Appalachia," in *Colonialism in Modern America*, ed. Helen Matthews Lewis, Linda Johnson, and Donald Askins (Boone, NC: Appalachian Consortium Press, 1978), 125.
10. Jan Davidson, "Introduction," *Mountain Homespun*, 28.
11. *Ibid.*, 29.
12. *Ibid.*, 31.
13. E. Carroll Arnold, "Appalachian Cooperatives: Economies of the Third Kind," *Appalachia* 11 (December 1977–January 1978), 27.

14. *Ibid.*, 23.
15. Whisnant, *Native and Fine*, 68.
16. David E. Whisnant, *Modernizing the Mountaineer* (Boone, NC: Appalachian Consortium Press, 1980), 167.
17. Whisnant, *Modernizing the Mountaineer*, 191.
18. *Ibid.*, 169.
19. Shackelford and Weinberg, 371.
20. *Ibid.*, 371.
21. Laurel Horton, letter to author, March 12, 1992.

The Machado Quilt: A Study in Multi-Cultural Folk Art

Kyle Emily Ciani

In the rural and nearly isolated southernmost corner of nineteenth century California, a Spanish woman grasped a truly American folk art—quilting—and gave it a home. Doña Juana de Dios Machado Alípas Wrightington of San Diego, created an appliqué quilt of an original design in the mid-nineteenth century. The term "original" may cause some quilt historians to question whether the quilt exhibits a unique form or represents rather an abstract application of a known pattern. This study explores the power of environmental influence in folk art themes and maintains that the quiltmaker, inspired by a pervasive, multi-cultural lifestyle, developed an original quilt design.

Her creation, known as the "Machado Quilt," has generated speculative inquiry among quilt experts since its discovery in 1953. Because Juana did not sign or date her quilt, debate ensues over whether to attribute the work to Juana based on family oral tradition, but nevertheless, experts accept her as the quiltmaker, have dated the piece circa 1850, and consider it the oldest known quilt made in California[1]. The special work surfaced in 1953 when one of Juana's grandchildren, Everett W. Israel, donated the quilt to the San Diego Historical Society.[2] Israel was the son of Captain Robert D. Israel and María Arcadia, Juana's second daughter from her first marriage.

Kyle Emily Ciani is a doctoral student in American History at Michigan State University. She devotes her research efforts to colonial and nineteenth-century women workers in the Southwest and Latin America. 627 Burcham Drive, East Lansing MI 48823.

Hand appliquéd and hand quilted, the "Machado Quilt" drew admiring accolades from both the novice and experienced quilt connoisseurs during the 1990 "Ho For California!" exhibition. Rich in color and composition, exact in execution, the "Machado Quilt" incites the historian to seek further information about the quiltmaker and the quilt. What images affected the design of Juana's unique medallion motif? Who taught her to stitch with perfection and flair? How does her quilt resemble other folk art forms created in the southwestern region?

As with most frontiers, California's history typifies the effects of diverse cultural integration that develops when a complex of societies contribute to the demographic. For California, these cultures included the variety of Native American groups with ancient lineages, descendents of Spanish land-owners, Mexican nationals, and American settlers from New England and the expanding frontier. Each group reflected distinctive qualities in their lifestyle, and as the area grew, inhabitants managed to maintain some of these social characteristics.

Native Americans indigenous to the San Diego area belonged to a rich complex of subfamily groups, and by the mid-eighteenth century shared "common cultural characteristics" such as food-gathering and lodging techniques.[3] A relatively peaceful people, they employed a barter system which enabled groups to supplement supplies through trade. For instance the Diegueño offered acorns, yucca fibers, and baskets to Cocopa in exchange for salt. Basket-weaving by Diegueño and Luiseño women ranked superior among the skills of these groups.

When Spanish explorer Juan Rodriguez Cabrillo landed in San Diego Bay in 1542, Spain became the first outside influence to exert its presence upon the indigenous people. From 1769–1821, Spain used San Diego as an outpost and Spaniards moved up the coast to occupy and settle the region with missions, presidios, and pueblos. Referred to as Alta California, the area attracted little attention from other countries and was populated primarily by military forces and Franciscan missionaries. Up until 1790, the Spaniards had to rely on the rough overland journey from Sonora and Baja California, to Alta California for their provisions. Ship travel along the

Figure 1. "The Machado Quilt" made by Doña Juana de Dios Machado Alípas Wrightington, ca. 1850. San Diego Historical Society.

coast began to ease their access and isolation, yet Spanish maritime laws forbade foreign ships to stop at any Alta California port, and Spanish ship travel proved inadequate to fully support the community. Forced to rely on a government quickly weakening in the world trade market, Spanish settlers eked out an existence by raising cattle and farming grain under the harsh conditions of unpredictable weather and soil depletion. The nucleus of settlements developed around the military Presidio (located within the area presently known as Old Town in San Diego) and the Mission San Diego de Alcalá, located six miles inland. By 1790, two hundred people lived near the Presidio.

Despite Spanish maritime law, nautical contact began to increase as trade ships involved in the Pacific route sought refuge in the San Diego Bay. Perhaps the first non-Spanish contact resulted when British Captain George Vancouver entered the San Diego harbor in 1793 on his return from his Pacific Northwest expedition. The first American ship, the *Betsy*, entered the port in 1800 to replenish its supplies.[4]

Although Spanish influence remained strong, when revolutionary troops in Mexico successfully overthrew the Spanish colonial government, the Mexican flag flew over the area from 1821–1846. During the period from the mid-1820s to the early 1830s San Diego experienced a burst of growth. The Mexican government relaxed maritime trade laws, which substantially increased access to and from the area. Visits from trade ships originating from France, Britain, the Netherlands, and Russia exposed the people to new customs, trinkets, and furnishings.[5] By 1822, whalers from Boston regularly stopped in California harbors, and San Diego Bay became one of their favorite spots. Fleet crews consisted of men from Africa, New Zealand, Australia, Portugal, Hawaii, the South Pacific, the Carribbean, and the British Empire.[6] Sailors saw San Diego as a haven because of its mild climate and excellent harbor, and soon they began to leave their ships to settle in the area, which contributed in large measure to a growing cosmopolitan community. Merchants realized relative prosperity by fostering trade reciprosity with friends in distant lands. For instance, San Diegan José María Estudillo wrote to his friend, Francisco de Paula Marin who lived in Honolulu, that he should expect a package filled with fresh plants, fruit, and a medicinal herb from Peru to arrive via a French frigate due to leave from San Diego enroute to Asia.[7]

In an interview with one of historian Herbert Howe Bancroft's agents, Thomas Savage, Juana noted that before Mexican rule her community had suffered from a general lack of provisions, but independence and increased ship travel made certain items, such as chocolate and clothing, available.[8]

Although no concrete evidence exists, contact through maritime trade could have been the channel for quilts entering the area. A review of quilt patterns described as native to nineteenth century Hawaii and Northern Ireland, reveal striking similarities to the "Machado Quilt."[9] Missionary women from Boston introduced Hawaiian women to quilting in 1820, and, according to Hawaiian quilt historian, Stella M. Jones, Hawaiian women created quilts as a form of expression rather than as bedcovers. Jones explained that they achieved their most common style with an interesting cutting technique. The quiltmakers cut a square design from material folded "diaper-wise, eightfold, the creases forming the corners of the border, the necessary seams falling at the middle of the sides. Thus by cutting one motif the entire border is produced at one time and with exact repetition of the motif." This method left a large and rather circular piece for the medallion which was also cut folded.[10]

Popular nineteenth-century Hawaiian quilt patterns typically employed a two-color scheme, and women most often chose to use red appliqué on white. Obvious correlations between the "Machado Quilt" and Hawaiian quilt design support the notion that activity between Pacific traders facilitated the distribution of quilt designs. Patterns originating from Northern Ireland also bear a resemblance to the "Machado Quilt," although trade patterns were not as direct between Northern Ireland and the Pacific Coast.

Yet another important connection between Hawaii and San Diego existed—Yankee Thomas Wrightington. Contemporary accounts date Wrightington's arrival in San Diego from Fall River, Massachusetts, around 1833. He came on the ship *Ayacucho* which would give him the distinction of being the first Yankee settler in San Diego. Wrightington opened a store which, according to

Bostonian Richard Henry Dana, offered welcome respite to weary sailors. In his memoirs, *Two Years Before the Mast*, Dana described the store as a grog-shop in 1840.

> This was a small mud building, of only one room, in which were liquors, dry and west India goods, shoes, bread, fruits, and everything which is vendible in California. It was kept by a Yankee [Thomas Wrightington], a one-eyed man, who belonged formerly to Fall River, came out to the Pacific in a whale-ship, left her at the Sandwich Islands [Hawaii] and came to California."[11]

The inclusion of "dry and west India goods" among Wrightington's wares creates another possible connection to quilts and quiltmaking in San Diego. According to quilt historian Sally Garoutte, dry goods primarily meant cloth during this period.[12] Moreoever, textile chemist James N. Liles has studied the origins of dyes and states that "available evidence indicates that quilting materials used early on in America were mostly imported from Europe (England, primarily), and therefore of European, Indian, or Asian origin."[13] Most likely, the cloth that Wrightington supplied to his southwestern customers originated from European trade to the area. Furthermore, the brilliancy of the red cloth used in the "Machado Quilt" suggests material that had undergone a Turkey red dye process. By 1600, Europe began to import large quantities of the "completely washfast and lightfast" Turkey red from Persia, and European dyers had perfected the dyeing process by 1700.[14] Because of its remarkable qualities, seamstresses highly coveted Turkey red cloth.

Perhaps even more significant to this study than the supplies Wrightington stocked in his store, was his relationship to the quiltmaker. In 1835, Juana's first husband, Damasio Alípas, died while serving in the San Diego Company of the Mexican Army, and subsequently she married Thomas Wrightington.[15]

Juana de Dios Machado descended from one of the oldest families to settle in Alta California. Her father, Josef Manuel Orchaga y Machado, was the first Machado born in Alta California, in October 1781 at the San Gabriel Mission (located near present-day Los Angeles).[16] As one of sixteen families recruited by the Spanish government to relocate from Sonora to the Royal Presidio at Santa Barbara, the Machado family continued northward to Santa Barbara shortly after Josef's birth.

Around 1807–1808, Josef, by then a corporal in the San Diego Company of the Spanish Army, married Maria Serafina Valdez of Santa Barbara, and he and his bride moved south to the San Diego Presidio. Juana de Dios Machado, born March 8, 1814, grew up with her eight siblings in the San Diego Presidio.[17] Times were difficult for the Presidio families as provisions grew thin, and Juana remembered that "the troops and families had suffered many privations through lack of clothing and other things, on account of the war for independence in Mexico."[18] She witnessed the changing of the flag at the age of eight, and cries from the soldiers of "Long live the Mexican Empire!" became etched in her memory.

Juana learned to sew at an early age from Doña Lugarda, wife of Alferez Ignacio Delgado, a sub-lieutenant in the Spanish army. Lugarda arrived in San Diego from her native Mazatlan, Mexico in 1819 and spent many hours with the young girls in the area. In her recollection to Thomas Savage, Juana showed her affection and respect for her teacher's varied talents by stating that Doña Lugarda was "very skillful in all kinds of sewing, artificial flowers, and other fancy work. The young Pico girls and I, and many others, went to learn all these things from her."[19]

Doña Lugarda probably taught the girls how to embroider using the *colcha* stitch. In colonial Spanish America, a *colcha* referred to a bedcovering—coverlet or quilt—that had been embroidered with geometric or floral designs with a long stitch that completely covered the supporting material (the *colcha* stitch).[20] Mexican folk art historians consider the *colcha* stitch representative of the beauty and skill in Mexican textile design.

At the age of fifteen, Juana married Damasio Alípas, who also resided at the San Diego Presidio. Her childhood friend, Isadora Pico, served as her bridesmaid, and the best man was her oldest brother, Juan. Typical of Spanish weddings in Alta California, spectacular feasts and dancing carried the wedding festivites through the night.[21] Juana's father built an adobe house for the young couple near the Presidio, and soon their family included three daughters—Ramona, Josefa, and Maria Arcadia.[22]

Figure 2. Doña Juana de Dios Machado Alípas Wrightington stands on the porch of her adobe in Old Town, San Diego c. 1893. San Diego Historical Society—Ticor Collection.

Figure 3. Doña Juana de Dios Machado Alípas Wrightington in her cactus garden at Old Town, ca. 1895. Desert plant life is native to San Diego and surrounded Juana throughout her life. San Diego Historical Society—Ticor Collection.

When Damasio Alípas died in 1835, Juana spent four or five years as a widow before marrying Wrightington, but few details survive about their marriage. The union produced two sons, Jose and Luis, and one daughter, Serafina. Wrightington died on July 8, 1853, when Juana would have been nearly forty years old.[23]

Throughout her long life, Juana maintained an intense devotion to Catholicism and eagerly assisted the local priest, Father Ubach, with charitable duties. Townspeople nicknamed Juana the "Florence Nightingale of Old Town," because she often accompanied Father Ubach into the backcountry to visit the Indian *rancherias* to aid the sick and help deliver babies. She also took in parentless children and fostered their care.[24] When Savage interviewed Juana in 1878, she had twenty-four living grandchildren and three great-grandchildren.

Living in San Diego exposed Juana to people from many countries with varying customs. Folk art generated in the southwest during the Spanish, Mexican, and early statehood periods expressed a blending of these cultures. To be sure, decoration in Native American domestic wares represents as strong an influence as European themes. Works display strong botanical and animal themes, and the "Machado Quilt" exemplifies these influences.

Truly captivating, the quilt has suffered slight discoloration which does little to detract from the quilt, which measures 62 1/2 inches by 82 inches. Juana whip-stitched two different solid red cottons onto a twill-weave white cotton to create a strong monochrome medallion design. The medallion simulates movement with the use of circular forms and flowing branch-like figures. Four corner motifs, which in modified heart shapes partially replicate the medallion, create symmetry. Four vine borders, one on each edge, add artistic interest, and a red binding encases the quilt. Each appliqué unit includes numerous pieces. Inconsistent lengths in the stems of the vines, branches, and corner motif patterns indicate salvaged material. Close study reveals that on two of the four corner images the maker used two different fabrics with pre-existing seams. Juana filled the quilt with cotton batting and used a plain white cotton backing. She complemented her work with a diamond quilting pattern.

Juana chose a red cloth so bright that 140 years later it retains its vibrant color. Juana revealed her interest in color, fashion, and detail when she described how the troops during her childhood dressed:

> [An] undershirt of cotton or other material—vest without facings which came down to the waist—of different colors—but the troops wore blue. Over the waistcoat went the doublet which was a coat with lappets on the sides—with red borders on all the edges—and with a red collar. . . .[C]itizens who were very few and the retired soldiers wore about the same, the color being varied by each according to his taste.[25]

According to Jonathon Holstein, "appliqué quilts reached their peak in mid-nineteenth century" and quilters seemed to pull their designs from nature, in both realistic and abstract designs.[26] Surrounded with desert plant-life, Juana could have designed her quilt as an abstract of the familiar cacti needles and rock formations. Did Juana envision an ocotillo when she created her medallion piece? Natural historians define an ocotillo as "an unmistakable plant, . . . composed of many slender, 3–4 meters long, whip-like branches which spread fan-like from the base. Thorns cover these green barked, stiff stems. . . . Panicles of bright red, five-merous, tubular flowers develop . . . at the ends of the branches."[27]

Close study also reveals distinct similarities between the "Machado Quilt" and images found in Native American designs and in regional religious and secular art. Basketry made by the Luiseño and Diegueño Indian tribes display the concentric and curvilinear movement demonstrated in the quilt. Graphic themes in eighteenth- and nineteenth-century religious devotions and vestments demonstrate the use of botanical forms and figures such as those found in Juana's design.[28] Moreover, similar themes characterize some types of Mexican folk art. Recognizing the origins and meanings of these images helps to understand how they entered into the region's art.

According to Mexican folk art historian Marion Oettinger, Jr., most Mexican folk artists, past and present, created pieces for utilitarian purposes.[29] Beginning in the fifteenth century, the Spanish conquest introduced Christianity to the native people. In many regions of Mexico religious folk art developed into a "syncretic blend of pagan and Christian forms," but the Spaniards gradually forced Mexican natives to concentrate on Christian symbolism in their art.[30] A unique form of folk art, *santos*, flourished in New Mexico from the mid-eighteenth to the twentieth centuries but were also found throughout New Spain. Art curator Robert J. Stroessner, describes *santos* as "distinctive religious images . . . or saint figures since they represent holy persons of the Christian faith."[31] Forms of *santos* included paintings on panels called *retablos*, *bultos* which referred to sculpture, and often elaborate altar pieces called *reredos*. Used for personal veneration in homes throughout Spanish America, *santos* varied in style due to available materials.[32] Areas with coastal access, such as California and Texas, usually imported products directly from Mexico and Spain, while the interior areas of Arizona and New Mexico depended on locally made religious art. Franciscan missionaries made the first *santos* in the eighteenth century during the early mission settlement movement as a way to clearly communicate Christian attitudes and beliefs to an illiterate people. The Mexican baroque style, which dominated the interior design of Mexican monasteries, and copper engravings from their books and missals, inspired their creations.[33]

Juana, an intensely devout and dedicated Catholic, probably owned her own *santos* which may have contributed to the designs on her quilt. Vines and flower forms on the wood and gesso *bultos*, La Virgen y El Niño Dio [Virgin and Child], resemble the vines on the "Machado Quilt." Property of the Mission San Diego de Alcala, this early nineteenth century *santos* traveled between the Pala and San Diego missions during the nineteenth century, and is representative of other local santos in this period.[34] However, only small groups of Indians and resident priests occupied the Missions by the mid-nineteenth century. In particular, Mission San Diego de Alcalá, located six miles from the Presidio, had been set afire by discontented Indians on November 5, 1775. Although the Mission was rebuilt by the following year, the distance between the Mission and the Presidio encouraged Presidio residents to worship in local chapels. During the 1980s, Mission restoration resulted in period decoration, and although it is not the original artwork, scholarly conjecture and subsequent research by a team of art historians formulated the designs which presently adorn the Mission and invoke Christian symbols of bread and wine such as wheat sheaves and grapes.[35] The Padre Luis Jayme Museum at the Mission displays artifacts from

Figure 4. Bungalow interior, ca. 1915, displaying excellent examples of southwestern Native American baskets. Note the curvilinear lines, particularly of the lower basket hanging on the right side of the hutch. San Diego Historical Society—Ticor Collection.

the eighteenth and nineteenth centuries, notably vestments, religious devotions, and baskets and pottery native to the area. For example, an early nineteenth-century vestment—of French embroidered green silk brocade with metallic ribbon—shows an elegant and intricately embroidered vine similar to the vine image in the "Machado Quilt."[36] To be sure, both realistic and stylized vine images were common in nineteenth century American quilts. This connection is meant to suggest an additional, not the only, influence Juana used to develop her design.

Santos vividly depicted the crucifixion of Jesus Christ and whether crude renderings or masterful sculpture, they focused on the human qualities of the Christ figure. As a universal symbol, the crown of thorns portrayed the emotions of pain and suffering. Could the medallion in the "Machado Quilt" be a crown of thorns? We'll probably never know because Juana left very few possessions upon her death, and, to date, we have no knowledge of *santos* owned by Juana.

Colcha stitch patterns also draw greatly from typically Christian symbols, yet were embroidered on wholly secular articles of clothing.[37] Popular motifs again included the lily-of-the-valley flower, vines, bunches of grapes, and a variety of flowers such as tulips and daisies. Sunbursts, sewn in both abstract and realistic styles, emphasized round or curved figures surrounded by vines and/or complemented by floral forms. All of these images resemble the "Machado Quilt" designs.

Still another culture could have contributed to the "Machado Quilt" design. Cultures native to the area, primarily the Luiseño and Diegueño tribes, also used vine motifs, curvilinear and concentric circles, and botanical symbols in the baskets they wove. According to archeologists who study Native Americans indigenous to southern California, the origin of a basket is difficult to place after it is removed from its geographical setting because all the tribes in the area shared similar design traits: elaborate geometric forms that emphasize the four earth directions, and use of concentric lines, diamonds, and triangles.[38] Southern California basket-makers either twined or coiled the reeds, then used juncas or sumac plants for color complements.[39] Sparse patterns using the "natural pale red or dyed black juncas on a sumac background" characterized Luiseño baskets. Diegueños, who lived in the Mesa Grande-Santa Ysabel region north of San Diego, created a deeper orange-red color from the juncas because of the naturally more intense red tone of the plant. Their designs, spotlighted with red, suggest movement much in the same manner as the "Machado Quilt." Baskets made by Native Americans were ubiquitous utensils used by everyone who lived in and around San Diego, so Juana would have been familiar with their design characteristics. Also, because she regularly nursed Indian people, she may have learned some basketmaking techniques.

From *santos* to utility baskets, the symbols, patterns, and shapes found in these objects suggest that Juana's design received creative reinforcement from a wide array of pre-existing art forms in her locale, as well as transplanted art, such as imported quilts or quilt patterns. An illiterate woman, Juana left no written records of her reasons for making this quilt or of its intended purpose, nor were family members aware of her intentions. Doña Juana de Dios Machado Alípas Wrightington died December 24, 1890, at the age of 87, in "comparative poverty" at the home of her daughter, Maria Arcadía Israel.[40] During her full life she touched many with her strength and charitable nature. When Savage introduced his readers to Juana he obviously respected her fortitude and accomplishments:

> This lady is the widow of the late Thomas Wrightington—never had an opportunity to acquire an education—cannot read or write, but is able to speak English quite fluently. She is quite intelligent, and conceals her age in the most extraordinary manner—is 64 years old and no one would take her to be much over 45—has hair as black as a raven's wing, without the slightest sign of gray. . . . The old lady looks healthy and hearty and promises to live to see her great-great-grandchildren. She has assured me that she never knew what a serious illness was, and never had occasion to call a physician to attend on her except to bring her children into the world.[41]

Juana's personal history represents the multi-cultural impact experienced by the people living in San Diego during its socially formative years, and her quilt is a tool for examining this diversity. As a part of the San Diego Historical Society's textile collection it will be cherished, respected, and shared with the community. A beautiful reminder of San Diego's past, the "Machado Quilt" demonstrates how each culture blended to create balance in art, and eventually, in society.

Acknowledgments

The author wishes to thank the curatorial staff of the San Diego Historical Society, particularly Registrar Barbara Pope, Professor Therese T. Whitcomb, University of San Diego, and Janet Ruggles, Balboa Art Conservation Curator.

Notes

1. Mary Hjalmarson, phone interview by author, July 5, 1991; and Jean Ray Laury, *Ho For California! Pioneer Women and Their Quilts* (New York: E.P. Dutton, 1990):33–34. The "Machado Quilt" represented one of the earliest quilts in the California Heritage Quilt Project exhibition. The exhibition included quilts that had been made in other areas and brought to California, therefore, some of the exhibited quilts were older than the "Machado Quilt."
2. Catalog Card No. SDH 53.1.2, *Curatorial Assession File*, San Diego Historical Society, Balboa Park, San Diego, California; and Ray Brandes, "Letter to the Editor," *The Californians* (May/August 1991): 12. Dr. Brandes is a great-grandchild of Juana's. In "Times Gone By in Alta California," *Quarterly Historical Society of Southern California* (September 1959): 195–244, Brandes translated his grandmother's reminiscences and provided an explanatory introduction and genealogical chart for the study.
3. Iris H. W. Engstrand, *San Diego: California's Cornerstone*, (Tulsa: Continental Heritage Press, 1980), 12–14.
4. Ibid., 22.
5. Iris W. Engstrand, "San Diego: Its Spanish and Indian Heritage," *The Cross and the Sword* (San Diego: The Fine Arts Society, 1976), 12; and Iris W. Engstrand and Ray Brandes, *Old Town San Diego: 1821–1874* (San Diego: Alcala Press, 1976), 5.
6. Ronald V. May, "Dog-Holes, Bomb-Lances and Devil-Fish: Boom Times for the San Diego Whaling Industry," *Journal of San Diego History* 32 (Spring 1986): 74; and Adele Ogden, "Boston Hide Droghers Along the California Shores," *California Historical Society Quarterly* 8 (December 1929): 289–305.
7. Engstrand and Brandes, *Old Town*, 5.
8. Recollection of Señora Doña Juana Machado de Ridington [Wrightington], Bancroft Library, 1878, translation by Winifred Davidson, April 1943. Documents File—Machado Family 1836–1868, Balboa Park, San Diego Historical Society, Research Archives, San Diego, California, 3.
9. Valerie Wilson, "Quiltmaking in Counties Antrim and Down," *Uncoverings 1991*, ed. Laurel Horton (San Francisco: American Quilt Study Group, 1992); and Stella M. Jones, *The Cross and the Sword*, (1930; reprint, Honolulu: Honolulu Academy of Arts, 1973).
10. Jones, *Hawaiian Quilts*, 11.
11. Richard Henry Dana, *Two Years Before the Mast*, as cited in Engstrand and Brandes, *Old Town*, 6.

12. Sally Garoutte, "The Scarcity of Textiles," *Quilters Journal* (Spring 1979): 5.
13. James N. Liles, "Dyes in American Quilts Made Prior to 1930, With Special Emphasis on Cotton and Linen," *Uncoverings 1984* ed. Sally Garoutte (Mill Valley CA: American Quilt Study Group, 1985), 30.
14. Ibid.
15. Recollections of Juana Machado, 1, 3, and 9.
16. Documents File—Machado Family 1836–1868.
17. Recollections of Juana Machado, 1; and Raymond S. Brandes, "Translation and Annotation of Machado Recollections," Documents File—Machado Family.
18. Recollections of Juana Machado, 3.
19. Ibid.
20. Marianne L. Stoller, "Traditional Hispanic Arts and Crafts in the San Luis Valley of Colorado," *Hispanic Crafts of the Southwest*, exhibition catalog, ed. William Wroth, (Colorado Springs: The Taylor Museum, 1977), 81–96.
21. Recollections of Juana Machado, 9.
22. Documents File—Machado Family. Birth dates for her daughters are unknown.
23. Ibid.
24. Ibid.
25. Recollections of Juana Machado, 5.
26. Jonathan Holstein, *The Pieced Quilt: An American Design Tradition* (Boston: New York Graphic Society, 1973), 122.
27. Jeannette Coyle and Norman C. Roberts, *A Field Guide to the Common and Interesting Plants of Baja California* (La Jolla CA: Natural History Publishing Co., 1975), 126.
28. Jean Stern, ed. *The Cross and the Sword* (San Diego: The Fine Arts Society, 1976). Pages 45–99 show excellent examples of Spanish colonial and Mexican folk art including a variety of *santos*, Church vestments, and colcha stitches.
29. Marion Oettinger, Jr. *Con Cariño: Mexican Folk Art from the Collection of the San Antonio Museum Association*, exhibition catalog (San Antonio: San Antonio Museum, 1986), 33.
30. Ibid., 15.
31. Robert J. Stroessner, "Traditional Folkart of Hispaño New Mexico," *The Cross and the Sword*, (San Diego: Fine Arts Society of San Diego, 1976), 20. Also, Robert L. Shalkop, *Wooden Saints: The Santos of New Mexico* (Colorado Springs: The Taylor Museum, 1973.)

32. Carl Schaefer Dentzel, "Regional Variations in Santero Art," *The Cross and the Sword*, 27, with clarifying notes from editor Jean Stern.
33. Stroessner, 20. Santero art reached its "golden age" between 1821–1860.
34. Stern, *The Cross and the Sword*, 32.
35. Therese T. Whitcomb, interview with author, San Diego, California, December 18, 1990.
36. Padre Luis Jayme Museum, Mission Basilica San Diego de Alcalá, San Diego, California. Three nineteenth-century vestments are exhibited at the Museum and the vine images embroidered on them bear great resemblance to themes in the "Machado Quilt."
37. Reynalda Ortiz y Piño de Dinkel and Dora Gonzales de Martínez, *Una Coleccion de Adivinanzas Diseños de Colcha—A Collection of Riddles and Colcha Designs* (Santa Fe: Sunstone Press, 1988).
38. Bernice McAllister and Christopher L. Moser, eds. *Rods, Bundles and Stitches: A Century of Southern California Indian Basketry* (Riverside: Riverside Museum Press, 1981), 1; and Catherine Hemmerdinger, "Design," *Rods, Bundles and Stitches*, 114.
39. William C. Cain and Justin F. Farmer, "Materials, Techniques and Styles," *Rods, Bundles and Stitches*, 86–87.
40. Brandes, "Translation and Annotation of Machado Recollections."
41. Recollections, preface.

Index

Page numbers in **boldface** refer to illustrations.

The American Quilt Study Group is a nonprofit organization devoted to uncovering and disseminating the history of quiltmaking as a significant part of American art and culture. AQSG encourages and supports research on quilts, quiltmaking, quiltmakers, and the textiles and materials of quilts. Membership and participation are open to all interested persons. For further information, contact the American Quilt Study Group, 660 Mission Street, Suite 400, San Francisco, CA 94105.